Working Like the Rest of Us

RICHARD SYMS

Working Like the Rest of Us

An Alternative Ministry

SCM PRESS LTD

The quotation on pp. 95–6 from John Whiting's play *The Devils*, published by Heinemann Educational Books, is made by kind permission of A. D. Peters and Co.

334 01808 0

First published 1979
by SCM Press Ltd,
58 Bloomsbury Street London WC1

Filmset in 'Monophoto' Times by
Richard Clay (The Chaucer Press) Ltd, Bungay, Suffolk
and Printed in Great Britain by
Fletcher & Son Ltd, Norwich

To Pat

who has taken most of the brunt

Contents

Christian belief is not a faith once delivered to the saints . . . it is rather faith looking for understanding, an attempt to develop a particular perspective on the world.

John Bowden, *Voices in the Wilderness*

The theatre is holy because its purpose is holy; it has a clearly defined placed in the community and it responds to a need the churches can no longer fill.

Peter Brook, *The Empty Space*

Communities need spiritual communication, man's understanding of man should not take place through books and media removed from real encounter. The theatre is the lay church. The actor is a priest.

Clive Swift, *The Job of Acting*

1

Working Like the Rest of Us

The title comes from our butcher. It had just reached the local press, and so the public, that the vicar was just about not only to leave the parish, but to give up full-time ministry and become an actor. The butcher knocked a couple of pence off the price of a pork chop, as he had done before, but this time he said, 'Well, now that you're going to be working like the rest of us.' It was interesting, coming from him. He was one of those who knew that I was not a priest who spent life tending roses in the vicarage garden. He knew that I took the job fairly seriously. He was one who would tell me about people on the estate who needed a visit, and he knew that I would actually visit them. He did not see me as a one-day-a-week vicar, invisible for six, incomprehensible for one. And yet when it came to the announcement, he did not regard the priest as 'working'.

And even more interesting, he regarded an actor not as the rarified, other-worldly creature of popular imagination, but as actually 'working', and, moreover, 'like the rest of us'. Maybe he knows that actors, like him, receive a weekly wage packet. If I had my own reservations that all I was about to do was exchange one idealist's dream for another, they were dispelled by that remark of his.

Other reactions to the news were more predictable. My wife, of course, had shown hers some time before. At first she was sceptical, and understandably. She had heard me say I was going to do it more times than I dare count. Nearly ten years before, I had written to a few friends in the theatre to ask about job chances, and had been successfully deterred, and she needed a month or so to be convinced that this time I really meant it. Once she discovered that I did, she had the same trepidations as I did, but there was enough to tell me that she was fundamentally in agreement, that the time had come to stop the clergyman's life. Both of us had always sat very light to the role and the status, and had been somehow fighting to retain our own personalities through them. A part of her began to express real relief.

My colleagues had known my growing dissatisfaction. They knew that it would not be long before I thought of moving from this parish, and they, no more than I, could not see me taking another church and starting the same process all over again. I don't think they were totally surprised. They knew that I had been chaplain to theatres and night-clubs for most of my ten years, that I was very much involved with the local drama group, that I did a lot of drama with the young-sters at my own church, that I had directed *Murder in the Cathedral* in the large parish church in the town, and a mas-sive Passion Play around the streets last Good Friday. They knew the thing was in my blood.

I knew that I meant it when I wrote to the Bishop. He thanked me for the work I had done, and went on to say that he had a feeling I was doing the right thing. And I think he meant it. The congregation had to be told one Sunday morn-ing. It wasn't easy, since the notice I was going to give was, of necessity, rather short. Jobs in the theatre come up at a week or two's notice, and I could not risk throwing myself on to the dole at the very start, so the announcement had to wait until I had a job to go to. As a result, I had to tell the parish only a matter of three weeks before I went. There was some shock, some tears, and there were some who knew me better who were not surprised, but even those felt obliged to predict that I would be back 'in the church' in five or ten years. It had to be carefully explained that I was not resigning my orders, only giving up my job, and that for the time being at least, I was remaining a priest, and intended to exercise some sort of Christian ministry in my new career.

And last, but not least, there was the media. The local papers, of course, gave it headline coverage. And within that three weeks, it was picked up by several nationals, local television and 'religious' radio. There was clearly an element of the bizarre in the idea of a vicar becoming an actor; all the 'actress to the bishop' jokes flooded to the fore. When I was sitting being interviewed or the cameras arrived at the church, I couldn't help wondering whether it would have been the same if I had been a gas-fitter, or if I was about to join a board of directors.

There may be a very simple reason for my decision – that I had just passed my thirty-fifth birthday, which feels like half-way, and that I wanted a change. And I couldn't tolerate the idea of sitting in a vicarage somewhere at seventy saying, 'I might have gone into the theatre. I wonder what would have happened if . . .' And I remember a telephone conversation some months before when I was telling somebody what I had been doing recently, and the thought entered the back of my mind that I was working a sixty or seventy hour week, and I wasn't actually enjoying it. And that was worrying.

So the decision was made, letters were written, people were talked to, auditions were faced. On Sunday, 2nd April, I conducted my last services as vicar of the church. The following day, I drove a hundred miles to a repertory theatre and began rehearsals for a new musical due to open three weeks later.

2

A Bunch of Last Straws

There were, obviously, I suppose, a series of events during my last year in the parish that prompted my decision. None of them were new to me, they were all arguments or issues that I had encountered before in other parishes. But somehow then I had the belief that things could be changed, that if one preached carefully enough, that if one related well enough, that if one set a good enough example of what one meant, that the priorities of a Christian community would change, that sooner or later the issues of the Kingdom of God would come to the fore. But now, after ten years, I was looking at them from a slightly less committed standpoint. It was time that I began to see things change, and if anything the battles were getting harder to fight than ever.

There were three events in particular. First, there was the Jubilee article. I have to admit that I misjudged the national euphoria that would be around at the beginning of June 1977. The material for the magazine had to be in a month before, so at the time I actually wrote the article, the Jubilee looked as if it might be a damp squib in any case. The article I wrote was by no means radical or anti-monarchist. In comparison to what I was reading in the national press, to the feelings of many people outside the church, it was excessively mild, almost pussy-footing. Which was why the reaction to it sickened me so much. The article was headed, 'No, I am not Willie Hamilton, nor was meant to be ...' (very clever, I thought, for those who knew their T. S. Eliot or had heard of Willie Hamilton), and I went to great pains to point out that I had nothing against the Queen or the Royal Family. I even made it clear that I was rather in favour of national celebrations, and extra bank holidays. But I ventured to doubt just how heavily the church ought to turn it into a Christian festival. Didn't it smack ever so lightly of the church taking political sides? And what about Christians who honestly didn't think the monarchy was a good idea? Did all Christians have to agree with the words of the National Anthem? If we were going to have Jubilee services in church, should we not also have May Day services, if only for the sake of balance? If good royalist Christians would not tolerate red flags in church on May Day, why should republican Christians tolerate Union Jacks (after all, it is also the flag of the National Front) in church in June? Let's, I believed I was saying, keep a sense of proportion.

The answers came back loud and clear. 'No jubilee in my church, says vicar' was blazoned across the local paper. I had, of course, said no such thing, but I knew that paper well enough. It saw itself as the moral guardian of the town, even if it had to make up its own news to do so. Words like 'disloyal' and 'peevish outburst' entered the letters column, letters from people who told me exactly what clergymen ought to believe, what God and the Queen were all about, but whose interest in the Christian faith clearly didn't extend to actually setting foot in church, or taking any active part in the Christian community. There began the obscene telephone calls, and the ones that were quite intolerant of any other view than their own, bits of the *Daily Express* pushed through the door

15

with phrases like 'Marxist yobs' underlined, and even letters from church members telling me that 'All Christians love the Queen' (French Christians? starving Third World Christians?), and another assuring me that 1984 was nearly here and Big Brother was waiting in the wings. (All I can remember about Big Brother is that his picture was everywhere, and that you were not allowed to say anything against him.)

And to me all this said that as a Christian clergyman, I was not allowed to have a sense of balance or proportion, that I either had to be a royalist, and it seemed a right-wing conservative at that, or I could not call myself a Christian. And the idea occurred to me, since I didn't happen to be any of those things, that the church was not a place for me.

Later in the year, the town churches had a survey on race relations. Many of the ethnic minorities saw the Anglican church as having no influence in their lives. The clergy sat round and wondered why. It strikes me that you can't tell them in June that the Queen is more important than the Trinity, and then expect them to believe that the church has anything to say to them for the rest of the year.

We did, unlike most churches, keep Trinity Sunday that year. When I read the opening sentence – 'God is sovereign Lord of all' – I couldn't resist whispering to the churchwarden, 'You don't think that's too controversial, do you?' Over those few weeks, the church and the public's expectation of it was clearly shown to me to be a right-wing, establishment animal, a total political bias, with which I was deeply out of sympathy, deeply in so far as it simply bears no relation to the priorities and attitudes of Jesus.

The second major issue was that of the organ. The church of which I was priest was not a beautiful one – it was a simple 1930s building, but had a warm atmosphere about it. The

16

organ had been installed a year or two after it was built. When we came to take it apart, we found it was a bit of a hotch-potch of an instrument, but it had served the church well for most of its life. It was beginning to cipher badly, not excessively, but it had a habit of intruding unplayed notes which wouldn't go away until you turned the whole thing off. The men of the church tried a bit of amateur rewiring, but it made no difference. We got some estimates for a rebuild and an overhaul. We were not a church with a strong musical tradition – the singing was always lively, and the children's choir was more than competent, but the worship of the place did not stand or fall by complicated settings or long anthems. Musically, I found the church all the better for that. But now of course we had a mini-crisis. The estimates all came in for something in the region of £3000. £2000 we had tucked away in things like Organ Funds and Fabric Funds, which left £1000 to be raised.

Now I come to think of it, it would probably not have been a crisis if I hadn't expressed my opinion. I relinquished the chair at one church council meeting, and pointed out as strongly as I could that half the world was starving to death, that £3000 could be a deposit on a mortgage for a homeless family, that I was sure God cared more about people than organs, that we had an unusually large number of people who could play all sorts of instruments and that we could make music far more excitingly without an organ. When it came to a vote, only one person voted with me. 'We like raising money for things like that, it creates a sense of fellowship.' 'People expect us to have an organ.' I said to one or two that this was for me a resignation issue, and my feelings were allayed by a vote to raise £1000 in addition for charity. That worked for me for a time, but I knew it was a cheat, and it clearly remained a resignation matter for me.

As I say, not a new problem. I remember objecting to £4000 for a church hall when I was a curate. £3000 for an organ rebuild is probably a flea-bite in comparison to the salaries of some of my church members. Two of the other churches in the town had just had their own fund-raising activities, one for money to build an extension, the other for £12 000 to replace a window. The large church in the centre was just about to launch an appeal for £45 000 for its bell-tower, organ and windows.

Sooner or later, somebody has to say that this is not on. The Christian community cannot sit there mouthing words about love and caring, while at the same time raising what to me remain exorbitant sums of money to spend on its own plant, on the luxuries it wants for itself, to project its own image. Church people enter into these things with gusto. Try to get another two or three to collect for Christian Aid and you have real problems. You can tell a man's creed by the stubs on his cheque book. The church's creed is self-preservation and maintenance of its plant. Those priorities are the exact, but exact, opposite of the priorities of Jesus. The only reason I sat back at the end of the day and let them rebuild their organ, and I said so at the time, was that after I had left, some other vicar would probably share their view of the centrality of organs to the Christian faith, and it might well then cost them twice as much.

The churches are now very adept at making the right noises – they can call it stewardship, they can say that we are building the community – but when it comes down to it, they are spending vast sums of money all over the country on shoring up their own buildings and institution; and every penny spent in that direction is a penny that is not going where it is needed. And I could see no movement, no shift of direction. Could I, as a Christian, oversee, share responsibility, for mismanagement of resources on that scale?

The third incident which tipped the balance for me was the Harvest Festival. I had, optimistically, set up a group of people in the church to take responsibility for mission and service. Together we came up with an idea for Harvest which we believed would help to make it a rather more relevant occasion. The tradition there was a church full of corn and flowers, some bars of soap and some tins, and all the harvest hymns. But we were a town parish. It struck us that the whole point of Harvest Festival in a village was that the whole working community came together to thank God that they had health and food, that the harvest was in, and that they were secure. So what was the equivalent in a parish like ours, which I don't believe boasted a single farmer? The idea was a simple one. The three morning services would be the same as ever – we were very much aware that you can't throw out all traditional observance – but in the evening, we would invite all the shopkeepers in the parish to lend some of their wares and hold a service of thanksgiving in the local community centre. A simple, not very radical idea, and it was, after all, only one service out of four. Many of the shopkeepers responded well. Many gave rather than lent their representative items, which we auctioned for Christian Aid. For a large number of them, the church had actually proposed something that was relevant to them. A lot of them were coming to a service of worship for the first time for years. Some of the elderly people who lived nearer to the community centre than the church were at last able to get to a Harvest service.

Meanwhile back in the church, there was a wealth of bad feeling. 'We've always had Harvest in church.' 'We weren't allowed to discuss it.' A lot of people, I was told, are very upset. If these people want to come to church, they can

19

always come. We'd be very pleased to see them. 'We like to have Songs of Praise on Harvest evening.' (In point of fact, I'd only introduced that the previous year.) And once again, it was priorities that was the question.

Just who is the church for? And as with the Jubilee, as with the organ, in practice I got the answer. It is for us, it is to keep our church full, and our members happy. It is to give them what they want and what they expect. The vicar can go on about making the faith relevant, about ministry and mission and service to the local community. We like him going on about those things – they make lively, controversial sermons that really make us think. But don't touch Harvest Festival.

The churches should stop having groups for mission and service; they don't mean a word of it. By mission, they only mean getting more people into the machine. By service, they only mean collecting an impressive list of what we do for each other. The whole idea of actually reaching out so that a whole community could feel the presence of Christ where they really were – that's all far too upsetting.

The whole relationship between the church and the community in which it was set was always for me the nub of the issue. The real nature of the local community rarely if ever seemed to impinge on the life of the church. I always felt a divide, and a tension of loyalties between the church-goer and the ordinary member of the community, and it was a tension that I felt should never have existed. From the church's point of view, you can see how it happens – there are too many other things, too many jobs, too many meetings to occupy the church-goer – we, the clergy, give them too many things to do, and so there is simply not the time to take on the community around as well.

Half of my parish was a large council estate. It was the rough end of town, and suffered something of an inferiority complex. The police were up there night after night. I took some trouble to get together the headmaster of the school there, the local councillor for the estate and the warden of the community centre, and we planned a weekend of dances and games and a fair and a parade and an evening in the pub, a weekend simply to help people to feel proud of living there. We sent out invitations to all the groups and clubs in the neighbourhood, and among them were more than a dozen organizations that were linked to the church. Of those, only one had the time or the inclination or the courtesy even to reply. Apart from a faithful handful, I hardly saw a church member the whole weekend long. When I challenged the church with it later, there were a million reasons, a million excuses, every one valid, every one convincing. But I could not help being left with the feeling that, for the average church member, the community that his church existed to serve came fairly low on his list of priorities.

My challenge, and the discussions that followed, did at least provoke a determination to take a fuller part if the weekend was organized again the following year. That determination was thwarted from on high. I left the church a couple of months before the second weekend was due to be held, and my successor was installed on, of all days, the first night of the weekend. The loyalties of the congregation were unnecessarily stretched, but then presumably nobody had pointed out that there could hardly have been a more ridiculous day in the year to drag everyone into church, ridiculous, that is, if the church cared about the community. But it doesn't, either at the local or ecclesiastical level. I happened to see the job specification for my successor. It was all about times of services, size of congregation, nature of the team ministry, spelt out in great detail. Just one brief paragraph mentioned the schools, the community centre, indeed everything that was to

21

be, or ought to be the real stuff of the man's job. I knew that if that man was going to be a priest for that community he was going to have to fight against all the other things that both his superiors and his congregation regarded as more important.

I had seen it all before, I knew what the church was like. Over and over again, I had seen everything sacrificed on the altar of keeping things as they are. As I apologized to the congregation for the Jubilee article, as I gave in over the organ, as I planned nothing radical in worship after the Harvest Festival, I could feel my integrity slipping away from under me. I either had to settle down and play this game along with them. Or practise what I persisted in preaching, kick away the crutch and get out.

3

To be a Priest

Christianity is, by definition, the religion of Jesus Christ. It cannot be anything else, and the life and teachings of Jesus must remain the test of anything that is to pass under the name of Christian. Variations on it, additions to it or subtractions from it may be interesting, may be arguably better philosophies of life, but they are not entitled to be called Christian. Jesus himself is not just a matter of doctrines; he was a historical person with his own ethos and atmosphere, an itinerant ministry, an almost random group of disciples, a conflict with authority, the hills and lakes of Galilee. And it is this from which the church appeared to me to be drawing away. To stop in the middle of a church meeting and suddenly test what I was saying and doing against the compelling prophet figure of the gospels became for me a devastating experience.

It was Jesus who brought me into the thing. Like many of my generation, I entered Christianity at the conservative evangelical end in my teens, through one of those 'independent' Bible classes of the fifties. The finer points of their particular brands of doctrine escaped me at first – I was drawn simply by the fact that I discovered Jesus to be the best man that had ever lived, that he was still somehow alive and had expressed his love for me. A certain arrogance (they called it 'assurance') deflected me from the trappings of that wing of the church, and I linked myself to the local parish church where I found others whose experience of Jesus was different, but no less real. I was one of that church's young people. We were, I think, a lively crowd, liberal but committed, and the relationships I made then have been basic to my understanding of human contact. At Cambridge, I encountered new things; the more Catholic end of the spectrum and, of course being the sixties, also the phenomenon that came to be known as 'radical' theology. John Robinson's *Honest to God* was the sell-out of the decade.

All that reached me just in time. I spent most of my time at university in the theatre, acting and directing for every group I could find – the ADC, the Marlowe Society, the Footlights. It had been my major interest at school, but only here did I have to make it match my Christianity. My Christian friends tried to make me musical rather than theatrical on the grounds, I suspect, that musicians were a nicer class of person. But the faith that grew in me then did not seem to need that protection. I discovered that I could be seen and known as a Christian, while at the same time being totally immersed in the world of the theatre. And the radical theology around Cambridge at the time was crucial, for it began to spell out very clearly that being a Christian was not a matter of going to services, or being at meetings of the religious groups (they bored me to death even then), but rather that Jesus was active in the world, was to be found in human relationships, that God had become man, and here he was, that he was love, and was to be made real in every human relationship. It was exhilarating and challenging. I often wonder whether I would have stayed a Christian then if theology had not taken that turn.

24

After Cambridge, at theological college where I was training for the ministry, being a Christian became, paradoxically, a much more difficult business. The old arrogance still hung on in many who were training with me. It became 'us' and 'them' – the radicals and the conservatives. We went to our extremes. We radicals became stupid and childish in our efforts to look like secular Christians, the conservatives asked us what the Lord had taught us this morning and went away to pray for our demise. Somehow the whole burning faith that had presumably brought each of us into the place was codified and reduced to issues of churchmanship and to the question of whether or not one went to Mattins. The guts of the thing was eased out.

I had a year's respite – in Switzerland – before being ordained, where I had one last chance to make real human and uncluttered relationships, and richly with people of many different cultures who were studying at the university there. A last reminder of the world where people did not care which churchmanship you were. I returned to be made deacon in the summer of 1968, with a view to being priested the following year.

I was unlucky enough, in retrospect, to have a brilliant first vicar. Others who were ordained with me, others who were curates alongside me, did not, and most of them left the church a long time ago. Mine was a priest of great humanity and integrity. He spent ten years in that suburban parish, and broke down massive barriers. He opened people up in an amazing way. He left towards the end of my curacy there, and the Bishop found it hard to replace him. Three priests turned down the job. A fourth took it (I don't think he knew he was the fourth), and in the space of two church council meetings reversed almost every policy that his predecessor had taken ten years to create. I left soon after. The new vicar may have been brilliant in his own different way. I don't know. But what price the other man's ministry? What price ten years of his life?

Very early in my ministry, I began to see that kind of thing happen. I saw arguments going on and issues being fought within the parish that seemed to matter like hell to everyone else except me. Should the choir or the congregation sing the Nunc Dimittis? The question took two working days to sort out. Thus when I came to be priested, I had some doubts, not about wanting to be ordained, but about the way it was happening, and the nature of the beast I appeared to be taking on. There was a dust-up at the ordination retreat because two of us had missed a service one morning – I was told that for an hour or so my career hung in the balance because of it. And when I was actually ordained in a parish church that I had never seen before, I had a compelling sense that it should have been my own congregation, not the Bishop, who had decided on my ordination, and that they should have performed the ceremony in the church where we all worked. I distinctly remember leaving the service knowing that it was an irrelevant charade.

None of these feelings mean that I had any regrets at all about the career I had chosen. The mechanics worried me, the hypocrisy I began to see appalled me, but the decision I had made was done with total conviction. Towards the end of Cambridge, I had actually been offered a job directing in the theatre. It was the chance of a life-time, and I had to make a conscious decision to turn it down. My immediate faith in Jesus had not diminished. Whatever the failings of the church, I saw within it massive signs of hope. Here, at least, the name of Jesus was being spoken, here there was a vision of what the world might become. I have no sense that I should not have been ordained in the first place. One close friend accused me of wanting to be 'the biggest possible fish in the smallest possible sea'. But it was resistable. I was a Christian, totally convinced of all the main tenets of the faith. However thoughtful the world, however good the good pagan, only the church openly declared that faith. It seemed a small sea now, but the local church remained a key point in the community. We could reach out and change things, we could build communities that set a vibrant example of how men and women might live. We could bring new vision and new hope to a society that was turning stale. The church could be a very powerful force in inspiring that hope, and as a priest I could be at the spearhead of that inspiration. I wanted to be a priest.

I celebrated my first mass with great pride. I used the young people a great deal in the service – they sang, they read poetry. The beginning of the vision. In no sense, I believe, did I fail to apply myself to the business of the vision. I received a great deal myself in coming as close to people and families as a priest is able to do. And all through the ten years of ministry I always knew what I wanted a priest to be and to do. And less and less did I find myself able to do it.

The last church, the one I left to go into the theatre, was not a bad church – lively worship, lots of lay involvement, a marvellous group of young people. It was not a stuffy place. Not untypical. And that was what scared me. For all we said, for all of my five years of attempting an honest, human, shared ministry, when it came to the crunch points, we still wanted to stay inside the building. And I began to feel that it wasn't me, it wasn't those particular people, or this particular town – it was something more profoundly to do with the nature of the church.

The church is an organization still deeply linked to the right wing of the political spectrum. It has as its main preoccupation the maintenance of its own machinery, and it is committed primarily to the building of its traditional patterns of worship. It should admit those things, and we would all know where we were. And those of us who are Christians, who happen not to share those priorities, can try to find some other way.

4

The Wider Issues

Once I had reached the point of thinking this, many of the broader issues which cause such discussion in church circles began to assume their right perspectives. It was not simply the day-to-day chores of parish life that seemed to have self-perpetuation as the main priority. Vitally important matters suffer too; for example, the ecumenical movement. We are all superficially friendly, but we are no nearer to real unity than we ever were. And the moment I began to look at it as a potential Christian outside the church, I could see why. We are not interested, you see, in making the faith real to the world, we are interested in preserving our own edifices. There is no reason, from the world's point of view, why the churches should not unite tomorrow. And the world knows that. That is why it has lost interest.

I remember the shame and hurt that I felt in 1970, when for the second time, the Church of England refused to enter into a commitment with the Methodists. I knew, I suppose, that it was only an attempt to shore up two dying institutions, but the refusal to do even that indicated very clearly that the church of which I was a priest did not even want unity very much. I have become sick of the confusion between unity and uniformity of worship. 'We'll all have to worship in the same way, won't we?' The answer was always No. The more relevant, more frightening question is the one that goes 'What will happen to my Catholicity/Protestantism/fundamentalism/ sacramentalism/the Bible/validity of orders?' (please delete those which do not apply to you). What I might have to do is sacrifice my own prejudices and brand of religion, and that is what I am not prepared to do.

In 1970, we tried to effect reconciliation between two tiny fragments of the Christian church. We failed. The love that binds Christians together was manifestly non-existent, and the church could never be the same again. If such proposals fail, as they continually do, the church can stop shooting off its mouth, because nobody is listening. Not a word about reconciling black and white, rich and poor, East and West, man and wife can be taken seriously again. The world is not that stupid – it knows rank hypocrisy when it sees it. If the church is ever to have any effect in reconciling the scattered parts of our world, then it has to be reconciled and very soon. There is no real division between the extremes of the church – they are utterly united in their arrogance and their conviction that everyone else is wrong. The 1970 vote was defeated by a uniting of the bigots. Most Christians would claim not to be so extreme these days, but I reckon that the very existence of different buildings and ministries in any one town carries exactly the same implication. Each church fundamentally believes that it is more right than the next one.

We seem to have drifted into a situation where we regard the unity of the church as desirable, but not actually necessary. We have forgotten that the unity of Christians is the declared will of Jesus and of the Bible as a whole. Our attitude to unity shows up just how obedient we mean to be. We have forgotten that the purpose of unity is 'so that men may believe'. Our unwillingness to be one is directly related to our refusal to engage in mission. Disunity is as fundamental a sin as it is possible to commit. The churches have become too used to living in the filth and slime of division. The sin of the church is so vast and so ingrained that it fails to notice it. Until it has eradicated the prejudices and minutiae of doctrine that divide it, it has nothing to say. Until Christians are together around the Lord's table, they have achieved precisely nothing. Improved church relations are quite simply not enough – what each church has to do is to enter the area where it hurts, where it costs something, where some prejudice has to be sacrificed.

Christians are nothing like scared enough of what they are perpetuating. The unity of the churches is not just a Good Thing of which we are generally in favour. It is what the church is about. It is life or death – and a divided, and therefore dying church is step by step taking God out of the world. Any church divided from its brothers is founded not on Christ, but on disobedience, laziness and a persistent refusal to love. Better no church at all.

There are too many vested interests. We get as far as we can without it hurting, and we call it unity. The church has all its people and buildings in bunches under labels in all the wrong places, and where the world is – in the factories and the schools and the pubs – where we could be together, where denominational labels do not mean a thing, we have next to nothing. The different churches are all too busy holding services and having meetings to keep their distinctive and irrelevant circuses on the road. Without unity, there will be no mission, and if the church has no mission, God will abandon it and place his trust in other people, other groups, those who are prepared to simply obey him. And the churches are left meaninglessly paying out cheques on a bankrupt account.

And the church will hack away at its discussions rather

31

than get on with what is blatantly the will of God. The same applies to all its other internal wranglings. In recent months, it has become equally obsessed with the issue of the ordination of women. Does it not know that the rest of the world has already reached the New Testament position of 'You are all one in Christ Jesus', that in most spheres of life, women are equal partners with men? And the organization that bears Christ's name is one of the few left that is trying to be a bastion of male supremacy. The argument that Christ's disciples were men is totally irrelevant – his was a different age in any case, and he certainly made no claim that they *had* to be men. The truth is that the church still regards the priesthood as status; it has not realized that to be baptized into the church is the highest status you can reach. To be consistent, it should stop baptizing little girls. The church should be brought under the law, and observe the Sex Discrimination Act. The endless debating is itself the church denying human rights that the rest of the world, under God, has already recognized.

At the 1978 Lambeth conference, the Archbishop accused the church of failing to listen to God. And yet a day or so before, he led the Church of England again to vote against the remarriage of divorced people in church. Most bishops know that they have to turn a blind eye to the fact that many parish priests are already performing such ceremonies. For years, I was one of those who did not rock the boat, and I offered the fashionable alternative of a civil marriage followed by a blessing in church. But the hypocrisy of that option eventually wore me down. What am I supposed to be saying? If it is wrong for second marriages to happen, then the church should have no truck with them at all. But if it is not wrong, as the very existence of these services of blessing makes clear, then we should go ahead and hold the marriage services in church. The other factor that made me abandon the hypo-crisy was that I was, for some reason, obliged to perform ceremonies for teenagers who clearly had absolutely no idea what marriage involved, while I was theoretically not allowed to marry older people who knew from real experience what the pitfalls of marriage really were.

The question is again theological – either the church believes in the possibility of forgiveness and a fresh start or it doesn't. There is no doubt in my mind as to Christ's mind on the question.

At all levels, the church spends hours discussing these secondary questions which a simple return to the New Testament and an ounce of integrity would solve very quickly, while the real issues go untouched. And when some Christians are given the approval of the church, and space in the church press, to complain about television programmes and mediocre poems in *Gay News*, while the real obscenities of starvation and injustice stare them in the face, then the time really has come to call a halt.

And it all comes back to the same thing – we are not interested in people. We are interested in ideas, in principles, in services, in buildings, in having a good, unruffling influence. But we do not care about people – the shopkeeper on the estate, the starving Indian child. We think we care. We mention them in our prayers – the divorced, the lady workers, the homosexuals even these days. But prayers are the begin-ning and ending of our caring.

But there is another approach, and this is the one that kept me inside the full-time ministry for so long. It is the cogent argument of all those liberal clergy who hope for the miracle of change, but who fail to see that by identifying themselves with the organized church, they are in alliance with all those things they claim to despise. It is the argument which says:

We care for each other, we are setting an example within a specific community of the way human relations could work. If they believe that, I can tell them from only a couple of months 'outside' that the world knows more about mutual caring than the church has ever done.

What we are creating within the Christian communities is not a model set of relationships. It is already an organization concerned primarily with its own self-perpetuation and precious little else. But for the individuals within it, both clergy and the more involved laity, we are creating even more dangerously a dependence on the church which is totally destructive of all their human potential. We have lost, it is true, to some extent, the awful Catholic fear of the priest and the fearful Protestant awe of the minister. Though only to some extent. But in the liberal, democratic seventies, we have replaced it by an equally savage inter-dependence. Churches vie with one another in introverted friendliness. They are now community-orientated rather than parson-orientated. But the net result is the same – good, often very exciting people, whose goodness and excitement is being stifled by the mark they must make within the Christian community. If they were not dependent people, they are by the time we have got them in, needing to be told they are loved. I have come to believe that the regular church member is unknowingly one of the sickest people in our society, and the clergy are the saddest professionals. They are people who cannot relate to each other without manufacturing the means of relating.

As a minister, my love for the congregation was continually being tested. To what extent did I visit them rather than the outsider? Would I complain if I was disturbed on my day off? How would I react when I was told that a good deed had been done? If only, I used to pray, I could set these people free. After the farewell 'do' at the church when I left, I came back

34

to the vicarage and wept as I had not done for years. Not because I was leaving, but for those sad, sad people to whom the departure of the vicar meant so much, who could not find any identity outside. And I was, maybe would remain, one of them. I had felt my own identity becoming 'the vicar', only able to relate under that label, performing the actions and words expected of me in that role. It had a safety – we all knew who one another were, why we were, where we stood in the ecclesiastical pecking order. And all the time leaning more and more on the thing, the crutch, the beautiful, inspiring crutch. But, as the Zen saying has it, still a crutch. Is there any way within the organization of kicking away the crutch and standing on one's own two feet? When I asked that in a sermon, I was told I was being depressing. For me, it was the most optimistic sermon I ever preached. I didn't know at the time that I was beginning to find my way out of the circle of dependence. There is a way of freedom, and it cannot be in the organized church as long as its major points of reference remain where they are.

To be a professional in the middle of the circle is depressing, once you have seen the nature of the circle. I became acutely aware of myself conducting services for only a tiny proportion, albeit a full church, of the community I lived in. I saw myself sitting on my backside talking for long sections of the day, discussing clergy matters – baptism policy, confirmation policy, maintenance of the buildings, minutiae of worship – on church committees and sub-committees. The amount of time doing the job that I came to do, relating to the community, inspiring individuals to search for God, was minimal. When in the middle of my time at that last church the town became a team ministry, the problem was increased: more meetings. Clergy team meetings took precedence, almost unbelievably, over the burial of the dead. Increasingly, I became bored out of my mind with the endless talk, and frustrated because there was no chance to be a Christian, either through sheer lack of time, or because of the resentment it would provoke. All this taking up a seventy-odd hour week, for £50 a week, plus a house which one could not afford to run, and one day off if you were allowed it, which was rare.

The clergy are not overworked. But they do have an obsession with work, make a virtue out of working all the hours God made, and the vast majority of the 'work' is of no interest to God or anyone else except themselves and the involved lay people whom they have cajoled into dependence.

5

Jesus

In almost everything, the sixties were an exciting time – in theology, in politics, in the theatre. A whole new world was just around the corner – we were really going to change things. It didn't happen. Looking back at the conservative/ radical battle of theological college days, it was a fundamental battle of attitudes to the faith, and sooner or later somebody had to win. They did. The radical theology of the sixties – *Honest to God*, *The New Reformation?*, religionless Christianity, the death of God, demythologizing, all that – is now regarded by the pundits of the seventies as an aberration and a blind alley. I don't know whether it would have been right for the church to take it on lock, stock and barrel, but its total rejection has meant some great losses for the church. Whatever its false dreams, it had drawn attention to some fundamental truths of the faith, which the church has now turned its back on.

The first, and most important of those truths is the doctrine of the incarnation. The churches have no such doctrine. They say they have, but in fact they are speaking of God dressed up as man, of a particular God-like man. They have taken up Robinson's phrase 'the man for others' and use it to cite Jesus as loving, but they do not maintain that his godhead and divinity rest in that phrase. They have totally failed to grasp the blasphemous enormity of what it has meant that God has become man. Man is now the fulcrum, it is only and always in the world of man that God will be known and discovered. The gap between God and man is closed totally, and it cannot be reopened. A group of people searching for God as separate from man may be on an interesting religious quest, but they are not incarnational, not true to the New Testament, not Christian. The whole point about Jesus Christ is that he actually was a man, a living, relating human being, and not a divine visitor. There is no way that this can be expressed too strongly. It sets the line between Christianity and its imitators. God is man, man is capable of being God, and once you have grasped that, there is no going back on it. There is no retreating to prayer meetings. Christianity is about man and man.

In the passage from the gospels that is read in most of our churches on Christmas Day appears one of the darkest, most mysterious phrases in the New Testament. 'The Word', we hear, 'became flesh'. It is also, I believe, the most under-rated phrase in the gospels. It encapsulates the whole truth of the Christian philosophy, and it carries the enormity of the Christian claims. Over and over again, Christians and non-Christians alike shy away from the truth of the phrase, as if nobody quite wants to believe, and we retreat into other ideas that we can understand, and that we want to agree with. Christmas is explained in safe, unscriptural terms like 'Jesus' birthday' and 'the season of goodwill'. And the more we clothe round the truth of Christmas, the more the real point that the Word became flesh gets hidden away so that we can avoid it. And to avoid it is precisely what we mean to do. Because the real point of the Christmas stories is too big, too frankly incredible for the human mind to hold. Even when we do get close to it, we get frightened because we begin to realize that the truth it represents is a shocking truth, shocking to the point of unbearable blasphemy. And when I say 'we', I refer not to the apparently religious, I mean 'we' the human race. The blasphemous idea of the human birth of God is a concept that offends the instincts and taste of all our traditions and upbringings. And so the religious and non-religious alike refuse to believe it.

Grotesque claims to make for one brief phrase. Let me explain what I mean. The subject is 'the Word'. Who or what is 'the Word?' In the legend of creation in the first chapter of Genesis, the universe is created not by moulding clay in divine hands, but in response to a series of verbal commands. As each part of the universe comes into being, God is made to say what the next part shall be. God said, 'Let there be light, sea, the sun and so on'. The picture is drawn of a voice echoing, and life comes to be in response to the voice. The Jewish people who invented the story believed quite fundamentally that God's command was not just an order to be obeyed, but that it was automatically effective. The voice was of itself the agent of creation, the principle of creation and the source of life.

The same principle applied to the whole pattern of Jewish prophecy. Each prophet began his declaration with the formula 'Thus says the Lord', and often ended with 'This is the word of the Lord'. The point of such formulae was partly to claim some kind of authority for whatever message the prophet felt he had to deliver, but even more to claim an actual effectiveness for the message, that whatever the Lord said was not only desirable or important, but was bound to happen. Once again the command of God was understood by the Jews as being effective by definition. Such declarations by the prophets implied not just something about the prophet, the nation and the circumstances, but also something about the nature of God. In the case of both the creation myth and the prophetic utterances, the Word of God is seen to be effective as part of the definition of God.

Whether or not twentieth-century man believes that about God does not matter. What matters in this context is what the writer of the fourth gospel meant. As he came from, or was at the least well acquainted with, the Jewish milieu, by his use of the phrase 'the Word', he meant 'God' and in addition all that that word implies, in terms of definition, of effectiveness, of principle. If he had used the word 'God', he would have been limiting his statement to a particular understanding. His use of 'the Word' throws the issue wide open. 'The Word' is at the same time God, the life-principle, fate, destiny, any ultimate value. It is a formula that stands for God, and all that the concept of God implies to human beings, whatever the implications are, whether concrete or vague. 'The Word' is God, whatever your understanding of him, and in whatever terms you define him, and all that your understanding implies about the nature of the universe and human life.

And 'the Word' became 'flesh'. The use of the word 'flesh' in the New Testament has prompted much discussion, mostly over the way that St Paul employs it, with particular reference to the moral condition of man. Strangely enough, the creator of this phrase uses the word very little elsewhere in his writings. It does not carry for him the moral connotations that it does for St Paul. Though this writer's use of language is rarified at times, 'flesh' is not a word he uses in a philosophical context, and when it is used, it is a basic physical word. Its implications are much nearer to our own 'flesh and blood'. For us, the word 'flesh', meaning human or animal flesh, is physical almost to the degree of creepiness. We do in fact speak of flesh creeping. In stories of contemporary cannibalism, it is human 'flesh' that we describe as being eaten. It is a word that in the right context and tone of voice can make us shudder. This is true partly because it goes against the grain of the way we like to think of man. Sociology, psychology, anthropology and all the great disciplines that embark upon a study of man prefer to think of the human animal as one capable of thought and reason, as a creature of ideals and aspiration, led by environment rather than instinct, as capable of forming communities, creating and living by norms of behaviour, setting up families and lifestyles. And just as the concept of death embarrasses us with its implicit denial of all human value-judgments, so do the mechanical features that lead to death. We shy off that definition of humanity that involves us in the mechanics of blood running through veins, bones that make creaking noises, the weaknesses and flaws in the bodily processes and construction, natural deformities, incontinence, and above all, the process of decay, the actual wearing down and wearing out of the machine. We cannot face death because we cannot face the facts about the human animal that death implies, the fact that flesh and blood is a mechanism that runs down, that apparently reduces our ideals and thought-processes to nonsense. 'Flesh' represents the incontinent, instinctive, weakest, most vulnerable aspect of man – the bit that can die, the bit that in extremities could be eaten. 'Flesh' is man, and all that man implies, all the facets of man that we understand, and all the facets that we try not to understand, and the word represents, too, all that our understanding says about the nature of the universe and human life.

And the Christian gospel states unequivocally that 'the Word' became 'flesh', that the broadest, most rational, grandest understandings of the divine creative principle and the frustrated, loving, decaying machine of flesh are somehow one and the same thing, mutually interchangeable, synonymous.

Hence our desire to clothe it around – nobody wants to posit any form of God that is synonymous with a decaying machine, no man wants to claim the arrogance of saying that this flesh and blood, frustrated and dying, is the principle behind the created universe. From strangely mixed motives, a kind of human pride and a kind of human humility, we bend over backwards to keep 'Word' and 'flesh', the implications of God, and the implications of man, as quite separate concepts.

And, ironically enough, it is in conceptual terms that the writer of the fourth gospel is thinking. Whatever the historical action involved, it is exactly these *concepts* that he claims are to be collided. In our efforts to evade the intellectual impossibility, we reduce the Christmas message, the doctrine of incarnation, to God dressing up as man, as visiting man, as pretending to be man. Such an evasion is, in fact, the age-old heresy of Docetism that the fourth gospel is written to refute. The important word is 'became'. The Word became flesh implies that the whole creative principle behind every galaxy under every sun became the whole human mechanism. To the ears of the pious, the idea is disgusting in every generation. Which is exactly why it was the pious who reacted most vehemently against Jesus himself. Whether the idea was around already to be personified by Jesus, whether Jesus formed it himself, or whether the early church read it back makes no difference. The concept of the total collision, total identification of the ideas of God and man remains ultimately blasphemous.

What the Christian faith in fact asks us to do is to completely redefine the words 'God' and 'man'. The pre-Christian definition of 'God', for example, really does carry all those connotations that we know so well – the God out there, distant and in charge, giving favour or not as he wishes, and who

wind up history and sort things out. The pre-
...ion of 'man' sees him as totally dependent
...ms of his creator, ticking along all right, a pretty
...reature whom, despite his failings, God will see all
...ht in the end. Over and over again, we have perpetuated
these definitions on into Christendom. For our own reasons,
we have chosen not to go through the process of redefinition.
The reasons are primarily those of safety and security. The
pre-Christian definitions hang on because we all know where
we are. We all know our place. God is in his heaven, and all is
right with the world.

Unfortunately, the definitions will not hold up in the light
of the New Testament. The doctrine of the incarnation is a
drastic change in the framework of thought. The Christmas
story itself presents something quite different. A new definition of God, defined as a squawling, illegitimate baby born on
a dung heap, whose brief life ended on a hangman's gibbet, a
creature of flesh and blood. The exact opposite of everything
we used to mean by God – not much of a god at all, in fact,
more like a man. And the Christian definition of man comes
out much the same – but capable of a degree of love and
caring with which we would not dare to credit ourselves.
Above all, man in the Christian scheme of things is capable of
rising from the dead, of totally overcoming what we thought
was the ultimate negation – not much of a man, more like a
god. Hence the total interlinking of the ideas of God and
man. Once the point of the incarnation has got across, it
becomes impossible to speak of God without reference to
man, or of man without reference to God. And we really
don't want a God-man. It suggests a god who is not in control, not as safe, not ultimately all right. And it gives man a
totally new goal, that has nothing to do with belief or moral-
ity. The new goal is to rise from the dead, to become God. If

43

one man got there, every man has a new responsibility, and we don't want to love that hard.

So we cloud it around. We maintain God as 'dressed up' as Jesus. Every Christmas, we sing 'Veiled in flesh the Godhead see', and reinforce our heresy. Whatever its original purpose, we use the story of the virgin birth to avoid the truth. Mary, we say, was his mother, but God was his father. He wasn't really man, he was different from us. God remains as he always was, and man carries no additional responsibility. And all we are doing is trying to qualify, modify, water down the central statement of the Christian faith that God has become man. Full stop. That God is man. Full stop. That, yes, in a sense, God really is dead, in that he had abdicated his god-ship. That he is man, living, breathing, corruptible, dying man. And we go on demanding to have God back where he was, so that we can philosophize, be religious, obey his moral commands. The Christian faith is believing that it is too late for all that. Man is now alive, and has real responsibilities and power. There is nowhere for him to run, no divinity on to whom he can pass the buck. The escapist's God just isn't there. William Blake's Nobodaddy, the puppet master pulling the vicious strings of life and death, was a creature of the pre-Christian imagination. Man has the machinery within himself for salvation or damnation, where he is, where we are, among other men, in the here and now. If all that is true, the Christian faith is not the simple dependence that we like to make it, but the grappling with a possible truth which is unsafe, bewildering and terrifying in its implications.

Jesus of Nazareth was an embarrassing prophet because of the blasphemous claims he made for himself and thus for man, and because of his total and profound disregard for the law and the lack of integrity in the religious and social climate. He was, and indeed remains, not what we expected or wanted. The blue-eyed figure surrounded by children and sheep is a total travesty of the historical figure. Dennis Potter was nearer the mark in his play 'Son of Man' with his coloured paraphrase – 'Render to Caesar the things that are Caesar's, to God the things that are God's, and *shut up*.' But I have, of course, omitted one other strain, which though it is the one that has provoked the 'Gentle Jesus' travesty, was in fact the most acute and blasphemous embarrassment of all. It is related to the refusal to condition, and its name is love. In the same play, Dennis Potter captured precisely how shocking the teaching of 'Love your enemy' must have appeared. We no longer find it shocking because we have reduced it to do-goodery, and removed all element of sacrifice. Love is in fact to be tested not by our social standards, but by the piercing love of Jesus. Again, in 'Son of Man', the atmosphere was right at the stunning moment, when Pilate removed the blind-fold from Jesus at the worst point of his humiliation. Jesus looks into his eyes and says 'There's no need to be frightened.' But Pilate, despite his position of power, is frightened, because he sees that the act of loving is more terrifying and demanding than he ever thought. And this was God. The points of human life where God is most active are where love is most active – the so-called 'rites of passage' – birth, mar-riage and death. They are the points at which feelings of love appear to take control.

And in the loving of Jesus, and the teaching about love by Jesus, the blasphemy rears its head again. God is man and human love, and nothing else. That doesn't degrade God, it merely means that human love is just a great deal more cen-tral to the meaning of existence than we ever imagined or wanted. Hence the command to 'love one another' is not a good or social thing to do. It is the principle on which the universe is based. Upon that principle, mankind is saved or damned. The whole scandal of the Son of Man is that he asked the God-worshippers of his day to look into his eyes, see human love, and say 'This is God.' There isn't anything else. God sent his son, and it turned out be a son of man, a human being in love. And it is unmistakeable blasphemy. Where we are, we know in human experience what it feels like to be loved so much that it hurts. We cannot bear the hurt. There must be something that will stop love overpowering us – suicide, divorce. We have looked in vain. The sin of Cain, the sin of Judas, was not in what either of them did. It was in believing that what they did prevented them from being loved, cut them off from the flow. And in that belief, Cain wandered the earth, and Judas hanged himself. But the search for an end to human love is futile. Because it is God. Nothing in all creation – and it's not for our want of looking – can separate us from the love of God in Christ Jesus.

So the second truth which is in fact a corollary of the first is that God is love. Where there is love, there is also God. When you did it, said Jesus, to the least of my brothers, you did it to me. That's where I am, in my brothers. A church which has no doctrine of the incarnation of necessity does not understand this. And so it has no doctrine of human love and caring, no sense of mission and service. If your God is separate, if he is not totally man, then all your loving in his name has to be from an ulterior motive, to make your own peace with this external God, or to get the loved one into the fold. But if God has become man, then human loving is there for its own sake. We just love because he loved us, because we see in other human beings the light that enlightens every man, and we respond to it with the light of God that is implanted in us, because we, like him, are man.

In a sense, that is all we need to know. The religion of Jesus Christ is the most amazing, freeing thing ever to hit mankind. No faith or philosophy before or since has elevated man to this level of responsibility and control. It means that man can walk free, without crutches, among his fellows, knowing that guilt and dependence are all over, that sin is forgiven, that he is part of the future of creation, that God has become him. Knowing that in every act of love or caring or sensitivity he will discover God, the meaning and purpose of the universe.

The churches have rejected all that, and for a very simple reason. Within a doctrine of the incarnation, and within an ethic of human love, the churches saw the seeds of their own destruction. If God has become man, and if he is to be discovered in the act of love, then the whole notion of a separatist community or a separate Christian identity becomes increasingly irrelevant. The organized church pours scorn now on the theology of the sixties. The names of Bultmann and Bonhoeffer and Tillich are not breathed in respectable church circles. Not because their theology is doubted, but because there is little theology of the organized church. The vast majority of mankind can rejoice, the only ones who need fear are the organized church. And so they have very simply closed their ranks. The protection, the self-perpetuation of the church is still more important to them than anything else in the world, even theology, even truth. So we have our teams and groups, our ecumenical discussions, our trendy publicity to keep the machine active and in view, to protect ourselves *against* Jesus, the God-made-man, who put human loving above religious organization.

The blasphemy of the incarnation remains at the base. The stinging pictures in the minds of the authorities would be Jesus curing a man of devils and saying, 'Tell them everything *God* has done for you' . . . It would be the taking of a child and saying, 'Whoever receives this child . . . receives me, and whoever receives me receives the One who sent me.' It would be visions like 'I shall draw all men to myself, when I am lifted up from the earth.' And the categorical 'Anyone who has seen me has seen the Father.' Look for God anywhere other than in the human face, and you are wasting your time.

William Blake was no more warmly embraced for the same doctrine in his time:

> Mercy, pity, peace and love
> Is God our Father dear;
> And mercy, pity, peace and love
> Is man, his child and care.
>
> For mercy has a human heart
> Pity a human face
> And love the human form divine
> And peace the human dress.

It is still quite unacceptable to the God-worshipper. And Jesus remains an embarrassment. We'll talk about anything – God or the church, but not about him. We'll put our base anywhere, in the traditions of the church, in taking the Bible literally, in getting involved in social work or politics, but not on a squat, Jewish, wild-eyed peasant who won't stop loving. He remains the stone rejected by the builders. The corner-stone that we refuse to use, and then complain because the building looks like collapsing.

This most threatening view of Jesus of Nazareth would be taken by the religious and the apathetic, because the claims, the freedom and the love look like destroying religion and apathy. Just one small group of Jesus' fellow-Jews saw those things, but saw something else as well. The story of the transfiguration of Jesus may or may not be historically accurate. But it pin-points the one other aspect of the man that has kept history's attention riveted on him. It is a moment of vision, a moment of glory. Its theology is unimportant, or rather it is only theology at all because it is related to human experience. It is an expression of that facet of humanity which

48

knows it is capable of the best – the Beethoven, the Donne side of our nature. The sons of men do have their highest moments, on the evidence of which they believe they can make sense of life. There are visions which take us to people and places. There are hopes and ideals. There are moments of love and glory. The struggle that we have is still knowing that they exist when everything points the other way. When Jesus got crucified, Peter and the others denied there had ever been a transfiguration, that they had seen anything, and they ran away. In the dark, or even more in the mundane, we will deny the visions, we will say we were always blind. Of the miracle stories that surround the historical Jesus, the vast proportion are healings, and a surprising number of those are about the opening of blind eyes. Such a moment as the vision of Jesus on the mountain is necessary to the blasphemy, because it puts the glory of God equally within the scope of man. What the church and world need to do above all is to re-capture the glory, the thing that made us tremble. We need to learn to live on the evidence of the high points. Man yearns to raise his eyes long after the experience, the vision has faded, and see, as the disciples did, no one but Jesus. And to see him in every-thing and everyone. That is when the blasphemy of God is at its starkest. God is man, and man is part of his glory. And it begins to feel like a way of living. It is God-man at his loving and caring, and also at his most evil. It is a savage coincidence that the bomb was dropped on Hiroshima on the Feast of the Transfiguration. But the very presence of appalling destruc-tion on that scale damns for ever the credibility of Nobodaddy, the God out there. If God is the puppet master with the strings, then he is evil. Glory exists in man's creative turning of evil back on itself. As well as love, mercy, pity and peace, the glory too is, after Jesus, to be seen only and always in the human face, as it was seen in the face of Jesus.

6

Death and Life

In the very act of protecting itself against Jesus, the church displays that not only does it not believe in the incarnation or in human love, it does not believe in crucifixion and resurrection either. If there is one thing that Jesus was blatantly unconcerned with, it was self-perpetuation. The whole point of the cross is that he was committed to the exact opposite, self-destruction, allowing himself to die, believing that resurrection would be on the other side, setting his face for Jerusalem, drinking the inevitable cup. Once again, over the last decade, the church has consciously and deliberately taken the diametrically opposite line, has decided not to follow its Lord. The one thing the church will not do is allow itself to die, to be crucified. Presumably it is not sure that resurrection would follow. Understandable, since without a divine doctrine of man and without knowing the absolute power and force of human love, it has no faith, no guarantee. If only I could tell them as they sit there, trapped in their collars and their churches, that they really have nothing to fear, that God is man, that human love works, that they can risk dying out, and that resurrection will really happen. Outside, men and women of love and integrity are discovering it all the time. There are free, joyful, human beings out there. God is throbbing through his world.

The cross, because it is part of the blasphemy, itself

redefines God. It also, it follows, redefines the nature of man. 'The man we once were has been crucified with Christ.' At the most simplistic level, it functions as an example. The first letter of Peter makes this point – 'Christ suffered on your behalf, and thereby left you an example; it is for you to follow in his steps.' The cross becomes a pattern for human living, and the principles of risk and costliness are written into any way of life that is to be called Christian. The cross is placed on the brow of the baptized, as a declaration that every baptized person is a potential martyr. 'Do you not know', asks Paul 'that when you were baptized, you were baptized into his death?' The followers of Nobodaddy set out to please everybody as well as their God. The followers of Jesus know the cost. Not all are in the tradition of Martin Luther King, but real humanity at least runs the risk.

The redefinition of man implies, too, a realignment of human relationships. In some ways, the writer to the Hebrews opens this question up in a clearer way than Paul. That writer takes as his parallel the divisions of the temple. At the end of the temple, hidden by a curtain, is the Holy of Holies, entered by the high priest, and only once a year, to offer ritualistic sacrifices for the sins of the whole people. That curtain symbolized a basic tenet of the Jewish system – that a gulf existed between man and God which was only crossed by a priest with a sacrifice. As long as that gulf remained, freedom was not quite possible. Even the priest had to beg forgiveness for his own sins, and all the failings of the people had to be measured by the annual moment of sacrificial cleansing. To set the whole system free, what would be needed was a priest of sufficient virtue and love that he did not need recleansing, and a sacrifice that, unlike the pieces of animal flesh brought into the temple, was capable of acting as a permanent sacrifice for all men in all times. The only possible priest would be God himself. The only possible sacrifice would be God himself. In terms of Jesus of Nazareth, the incarnation provides the priest, and the cross provides the sacrifice. Jesus acts as both priest and victim within the sacrificial order of things. The effect of the God-man is to open the way into the Holy of Holies. Though the image is drawn by this writer from one particular religious system, it is a symbol of the destruction of all religious systems. The curtain of every system, the curtain that creates the man-God gulf that is always present in human consciousness, is in effect ripped away, and we are presented with what the writer calls 'the new living way he has opened to us through the curtain, the way of his flesh'.

The cross opens the gulf for ever. It collides God and man in a single ridiculous movement. Matthew's gospel, written with a Jewish audience in mind, actually has the curtain in the temple torn down the middle at the moment of the death of Jesus. As long as the gulf exists, men are not free to accept anything, since along with the gulf, there exist fear and guilt and duty. The pre-Christians erect the curtain for their own reasons. But its tearing down sets up a life-style that is new, in so far as it is set in a new context. The days of attempting to appease an angry God are over. That would only be Nobodaddy. That is the God attacked by the atheist. But he never existed anyway. The cross turns the theoretical concept of incarnation into a 'new living way', a way, a context of living.

The writer to the Ephesians, who may or may not have been Paul, makes the same point for those outside the Jewish schemata by the use of the word 'reconciliation'. The same fundamental division in men's minds is still that between themselves and God, described here as 'a world without hope, and without God'. The cross becomes an expression of the ultimate reconciliation. It is not possible to see God as man, suffering and dying, and still maintain a distance between man and God. If all the talk about God does not ring true, Isaiah's vision of the distance may be nearer to human experience:

> Justice is far away from us, right does not reach us;
> We look for light but all is darkness,
> for the light of dawn, but we walk in deep gloom.
> We grope like blind men along a wall,
> feeling our way like men without eyes;
> we stumble at noonday as if it were twilight,
> like dead men in the ghostly underworld.

And, according to Ephesians, God does four things about it – first, he 'kills the enmity'. He takes the guilt of all parties, all sides in every dispute upon himself, thus making division between them a logical impossibility. Next, he 'annuls the law', that is to say, he takes away the book of rules. No rule of life could have prevented the cross from happening, and that is part of its definition. Guilt is impossible, because there is no cause for guilt. Third, he himself acts as the corner-stone of the new building, so that in terms of sheer human relationship, men are not divided, but rather cemented together. Men cease to be puppets who obey the whims of Nobodaddy, but bricks alongside Jesus. Take away the corner-stone and the whole thing falls to pieces. And last, he 'creates a single new humanity', a wholly different life, a redefinition of man, something much more akin to what Jesus meant by the 'true self'.

It is in this last that the test will come. Because I have been using the images selected by the New Testament, the whole process is in terms of what God does for man. But in the context of incarnation, we are also speaking of what man does for himself. The validity of the whole event will not be in speculation at any level, but in a distinctive way of living, a new humanity, finding its meaning within itself. It will not be a humanity apart from the world – that would be merely a return to the pattern of division – but it will be distinctive. It will be notable for its integrity, it will be humanity accepting the fear of meaninglessness as part of itself, because it is set free to be its true self. There will be no element of shamming, of playing, of pretending that the fear is not there. It will be a humanity that looks reconciled, a humanity where men and women can take each other's hands, look into each other's eyes and say 'Peace'. It will be evidently free of the law. The vision of the cross is there, with its scandals, its humility, its sordid, dirty view of God, to set men free to be themselves. This is the root and nature of man at peace in his environment. The writer to the Ephesians sets peace as the precious stone in its setting – 'He is himself our peace.' Peace, rooted in reconciliation, is the word spoken from the cross to the fear of man that it might all come to nothing. It has already all come to nothing, and the word that echoes is still 'Peace'.

There is one other element in the redefining of man achieved by the cross, and that is to do with time. Along with the fear of meaninglessness man has an obsession with regrets for the past, and with the effects of the past. Much contemporary literature is fascinated with the idea of what the past does to the present. Pinter's play *Old Times* is about a married couple re-creating a relationship from the past in order to watch its tinkering effect on their present state. It is no coincidence that the age beyond the war and the dream has a soft heart for all things past. Nostalgia – in music, in films, in art – has become a delicate fashion. It is only a new form of the continual human wish to start all over again. It is a reframing of every sentence which begins with the words 'If only . . .' It is a re-iteration of the phrases 'Like it used to be' and 'What might have been'. It is something wistful and sad at the root of humanity. It is a condition that needs to be accepted not with words, but at the level of feeling. We require a sensation that the past cannot impinge upon the present, though it may be looked at. Sacramental confession retains a place in the pattern of the gathered community, because it can create just this sensation – of a past dead and gone, of a slate wiped clean. Only the sure knowledge, the certainty of feeling, that the past is dead, gone, forgiven can set men free to live in the present, for the moment, which is of the essence of the new humanity. The motive for living is the act of living in the here and now. The contemporary encounter group can only consider the question of the behaviour of the group in the here and now, if it can come to terms with the deadness of the past.

The cross redefines man in the sense that the way to God is open for ever and the past is gone for ever, that for man, only the now matters. Man is set the challenge of a costly exhilarating refusal to live in the past, and to serve the God who has always defined himself in terms of living men – Abraham, Isaac, Jacob – the God of the human present.

There are two forms of theology. One is world-denying. It says the world and humanity are naturally evil and stand in need of redemption. It is the theology of the Old Testament, of the bias on the bowls, of established religion, of Nobodaddy. It works and breeds on fear and guilt and need. It is amazingly popular, though chiefly with the inadequate, and those who wish to reach a spiritual state by sucking up religion like a sponge. The other theology is world-affirming. It starts 'God so loved the world . . .' It believes in man, his world and its potential. It is that of the New Testament, of Jesus, of the cross. It is high time that the second had no truck with the first, and stopped trying to absorb it into the system of the new humanity. The two theologies are incompatible, there can be no marriage or cohabitation. The new covenant has replaced the old, it has rendered it old and, as the writer to the Hebrews rather coquettishly remarks, 'anything that is old and ageing will shortly disappear'. 'We have the faith', he goes on, 'to make life our own.' And it is our own that it is meant to be.

A world-affirming theology is the only acceptable premise for anyone taking Jesus of Nazareth seriously, and it stands in direct contrast to almost every other philosophy of life. It has one great difficulty. That difficulty does not justify any retreat to the sinful-man-crawls-to-holy-god pattern. But it needs looking at. I refer to the difficulty of the problem of suffering. It is the one question to which the Christian faith has no direct answer. When, as a parish priest, I conducted the funeral of a child, I was surrounded by questions, from the parents, yes, but also within myself. And I know that to these questions there are no answers. But at least, within the new humanity, in a theology that affirms the world, in the light of the cross, there is an understanding. It is not an answer, but at least it has nothing to do with the vicious cycle of cause and effect posited by those left in the system with no doctrine of incarnation. For at least here there is no problem of relating a remote God to present human pain and grief. In fact, to some extent it is only a problem at all because we have perpetuated the worship of such a god. The Jesus-god who was crucified is at least a participant, and not a watcher from the side-lines. There is no hell for man that is not hell for God, too. Since God is man, it cannot be otherwise. The cross persists, not only because love persists, but also because suffering, too, is eternal. The world is the cross in that it is the place where God chooses to demonstrate himself, to share the sufferings of all men, believers or not, to give men hope in knowing what potential for love they all have. Men suffer, but God is man. Evil is met by love, the conflict still rages, but is of itself the ground for the hope of the universe. It is the revealing of the sons of God, as the cross was the revealing of the first Son of God, Son of Man.

The cross goes on in the crucifixion situations of the world. As I write, they might mean Rhodesia or Northern Ireland. But only in crucifixion are the seeds of new life. That is why those who discover new life are impulsively drawn to feed it into such situations. Those who do not share or inject new life have clearly never discovered it.

The battle to be human is the battle against death in all its forms – in oneself, in people we know, in the church, in the world, wherever it is and whatever form it takes. To be human is to usher in life. A follower of the way of Jesus is not to be defined by his church attendance, or his saying of prayers, or his kindness to others. He is to be defined by the degree to which he is alive, and ushering in life. The faith of resurrection is about life before death, life as it really is, and a persistent desire to make that life worth living. It is about power, and force, and vision, and excitement. It is about reasons for being alive. It is the Jesus of visions in the Book of Revelation saying to a world in fear – 'Do not be afraid, I am the living one. I was dead, and now I am alive for ever.'

Jesus was human, and something happened to him two thousand years ago. Only a true assessment of his humanity makes it possible to take the next step and say that what happened to him could equally well happen to the human race, and each individual within it where he is. And the true human is there to ensure that it happens to his world and his environment. It is a question of the value that one puts on the sheer fact of human life, of its potential for change and re-creation. Today, they say, is always the first day of the rest of one's life. That is the spirit of resurrection.

What we have in Jesus of Nazareth is, I believe, first and foremost, a human life, a historical figure alongside other historical figures. The distinctive feature about him is that his human life was of sufficient power to render his death ineffective, both physically and in any other sense. I doubt whether the question of his being divine, of his being in any way directly identified with God, seriously arose until after the disciples realized the ineffectiveness of his death. Jesus' own claims, even if we are able to discover them correctly, are more concerned with the nature of man. He does not himself preach a doctrine of incarnation as an act of God. The chances are, of course, immense that we cannot discover his teaching in this area anyway, since every word of every account was written down after the resurrection experience, in the light of it. A group of people witnessed this particular human life, encountered this experience of him after his death, and then looked back, as it were, and with hindsight, put a value-judgment on him that made him worthy of the name 'God'. The gospels are written with that value-judgment already made. Even the incarnational statement that 'God is man' would not have been possible without it. The theology of the New Testament works backwards – the experience of the risen Christ puts a value on the life of Jesus, which then puts his teaching and life-style into perspective. From that comes the realization that what has apparently happened is that God and man have become interfused ideas. It is from the resurrection onwards that men knew in experience that they did not know whether they were talking about God or man.

The theory smacks of adoptionism, the idea that Jesus became God rather than was God. Attacks on adoptionism in this sense are only playing with words and time-scales. Having become God, the man is called God, and so is God, and always was God. All we are talking about is the point at which men realized that this was what God was always about. And it is certainly the order in which the New Testament works.

The one feature about a god as opposed to a man is that he is worthy of worship. There is no question of worship of Jesus until after the resurrection. When in John's gospel, Mary of Magdala meets Jesus, having mistaken him for the gardener, and Jesus speaks her name, Mary calls him 'Rabbuni'. The writer tells us that this word means 'Master'. He fails to tell us that the word also means 'God'. In other words, what is happening here for the first time is more than just recognition of the risen Christ, but actual worship of him. It is the same force which sends the women running away in fear at the end of Mark's gospel. The so-called Messianic secret is very much part of that gospel – at several stages, Jesus tells those with whom he comes into contact not to tell anyone what they know of him. The turning point comes when at Caesarea Philippi, Peter makes the explicit declaration 'You are the Christ, the Son of the living God.' From that moment on, the disciples and the reader are in on the secret of the true nature of God and man, but it is not until the discovery of the empty tomb that it ceases to be a secret at all. The awe of the frightened women is their realization that man has become God – their fear is a symbol of the worship due to this man.

The same order of events is the core of the teaching of the apostles. Peter's first sermon, in Luke's version in the Acts of the Apostles, describes Jesus primarily as a man – 'I speak of Jesus of Nazareth, a man singled out by God ... you used heathen men to crucify and kill him ... But God raised him to life again. David died and was buried – the Jesus we speak of has been raised by God.'

The operative word is 'but'. Up to that point, there is essentially no difference between Jesus and, say, David. Both are individual men who believed themselves chosen by God to fulfil a specific function. The difference comes with the resurrection – when the followers discover that this Jesus was not only called by God, but fit to be seen as God himself.

The most explicit theological statement comes in Paul's letter to the Romans, where he states what he regards as the main tenet of the faith. 'About his Son – on the human level, he was born of human stock.' The starting-point is Jesus the man, with no hint of divinity. That sentence shows moreover that Paul knew nothing of the legends of virgin birth. As in most of the New Testament, Jesus' parents were Joseph and Mary, human stock, and that is all there is to it. But, Paul goes on to explain, 'he was declared Son of God by a mighty act in that he rose from the dead'. It is that act that makes him God. It is not in fact adoptionism, and Paul is careful to use the word 'declared'. The resurrection is the point at which we discover and are able to declare the truth about God and man as it has always been.

The resurrection, like the incarnation, is a doctrine of man. We are not just speaking of a man come back from the dead – that would be a form of spiritualism. As God is man, so it is Man that becomes God, it is Jesus as Representative Man. It is humanity in principle that has defeated death. The concept of God-is-man is blasphemous, but marvellous. The process of the death of God is the establishing of the nature of human love. But it is only the risen Christ that is worthy of worship, only the resurrection of man that opens the gate to a living philosophy of man.

And the pivot question becomes the one that Jesus asks of Peter after breakfast – 'Do you love me?' The pre-Christian answer is immediately to hand – 'Of course we love Jesus, week after week, we've been taught to do so, it is part of our tradition, God has been good to me . . .'

And Jesus asks again, 'Do you love me?' And the question becomes hurtful to us as it did to Peter, because it slowly dawns on us that it is not a question about heritage or religious observance or the spiritual life, but about human loving, about the fear of meaninglessness, about mutual care and support, about meeting needs, about cost and risk and sacrifice, about being bound and taken to the rock-bottom, the zero-point where man would rather not go, and discovering there that man's hope and divinity rests on the question 'Do you love me?' The answer to the question is inevitably 'Yes', but Jesus' reply remains 'Feed the sheep' – Prove it and accept the cost.

God is man and man is God are true statements. But like all the truths of theology, they are true in the reality of human experience or they are not true at all.

With no doctrine of incarnation, crucifixion, resurrection or love, is there anything left of Jesus in the church? Maybe it was not just a feeling of separation between Jesus and the organization. Maybe it is really true that they are irreconcilable factors. The church can mouth the great doctrines of the faith, but in practice, with its heart, with its blood, it denies almost everything that Jesus stood for. The organized church now, and probably not for the first time in its history, represents all that Jesus lived to attack, what he died to destroy. Now we need those who will not press with charity for a 'religionless Christianity', but prophets who will declare that organized religion is the antithesis of the faith of Jesus.

'Organized' is the key word. One of the more remarkable features of Jesus of Nazareth is that, although he changed the course of history, he never wrote a single word, never founded an organization, never formulated a single creed. He has only inverted things to say about status and heirarchy. All authority is committed to him. His approach to law was broad and flexible. In other words, any structuring, any organization of his thinking is bound to lead in the opposite direction. It is in the very nature of the major doctrines of the faith at which we have looked that they cannot be organized. They are about life and love and death and hope. The only people who will try to organize those things will be those who cannot discover them for themselves, those who cannot relate without constructing a means of relating.

Some people think of Jesus as the first communist. That is wrong. Whoever pushed the 'Marxist yobs' clipping through the vicarage door was wrong. I could never be a Marxist for exactly the same reasons. It would be nearer the truth to say that Jesus was the first anarchist. 'Anarchy' is a word that is being obscenely misused by the media at present. It is used only and always with reference to violent revolutionaries carrying out meaningless acts of sabotage on innocent people. But they are not anarchists at all, they are organized, they are seeking to impose their own systems. The anarchist rejects organization and systems; he has to be pacifist, he just lives and loves by the lights inside him. Organization was the knife that long ago cut the church off from its living head.

There has to be, there is already, there will be a Christian alternative.

7

Home from Home

Theologically, these were the reasons why I took the decision to come out of full-time ministry. Within the organized church, the pre-Christian worship of Nobodaddy appeared to me to be written in, and the very truths which, if they had not made me a Christian, had at least kept me one, were truths which I found increasingly less declared or lived out. I left with sadness, but with goodwill. I remembered a poem that had appeared in *New Christian* many years ago, which ended

> But somewhere between the hymns
> I caught a glimpse,
> And that was enough.

I wrote in the parish magazine that I still saw within facets of the community I was leaving signs of hope, and explained that I did not in any sense see myself as leaving the church, but rather looking for a new way to make its ministry effective. I left with a certain warmth and confidence, the same confidence with which I became ordained, the confidence of what the church might become. I had come to believe that it was not performing its social role, that it was wedded to pre-Christian theology, but I wanted to believe still that its heart was warm, that its talk of caring and fellowship at least was not empty rhetoric.

The weeks that followed my resignation to some extent shattered that last illusion. We were, as I said, a team ministry. Though it was protocol not to inform the congregation of my departure until a date was fixed (such are the open relationships within the Christian community), I did, out of a sense of loyalty to my colleagues, feel obliged to share my intentions with them some months before. And on our side we began to look for somewhere to live. That last task was a great deal harder than we expected. But it was not made easier by bumbling inefficiency from the church. There was a muddle over the date by which we were to leave the vicarage. I knew that we were only staying there after I had finished work by the generosity of the team, but I did expect a clear date by which we were to leave, I had expected a month or so's notice, and I certainly expected that somebody would care whether or not we had anywhere to live. None of that happened. At the end, we found ourselves with two weeks notice. I, of course, as was well known, was by this time working a hundred miles away, only home on Sundays, which meant that for me it was effectively two days' notice. A date had apparently been set earlier, but it hadn't actually reached us. My wife, of course, had the full two weeks, and virtually single-handed packed up an entire four-bedroomed house, working till four in the morning most nights, and on tablets from the doctor to keep her sane. And still with nowhere to go. When we moved out, we were simply homeless. And, interestingly enough, my successor was not moving in for another month. While we were on the streets, scrounging for a bed, the house was being redecorated. It was not so much the facts that made me so angry, as the utter lack of human caring. Three or four times a week, my colleagues on the team came to take services at what had been my church. The church stood right next door to the vicarage. Not once did one of them call in to see how my wife was coping, let alone offer any practical help.

On the second Sunday, we got all the furniture into store with help from some kind friends – from the local drama group, and a few 'fringe' members of the congregation. Needless to say, not one of my brother clergy lifted a finger. I remembered with irony that one of them had said at the meeting some months back when I expressed my intentions that, from his experience as a council youth worker, it was necessary to have a Christian support group if one also wanted to exercise one's priesthood. And within weeks of leaving, it was our barely Christian friends who did the work. My mental and psychological support came from my new colleagues, those in the theatre, who always bothered to ask how we were, asked after my wife. One offered to drive out from London to help us, another offered us the use of his van. There are a large number of rich, caring people around. But the irony was that it was they who provided the support against the incompetence and unwillingness of the church.

The furniture went into store, the cat to a cattery, and we to furnished rooms around the corner. Still in the parish, but outside the scope of the church's caring. I tell the story now with no particular bitterness; I am not certain I have any right to that. Rather with sadness. I hold no particular personal resentment against the individuals involved. They are very sad people, and I pity their inability to relate in any sensitive way. And, after all, I had been one of their number.

One of my new colleagues at the theatre had asked me how things were going. It's amazing, I said, that I should be so surprised. I have known for ten years or more that the church treats people like this. 'You mean,' he said, 'that you've done it to other people yourself?' My hackles rose, and he saw it.

He assured me that he was only joking. Maybe he was, maybe he wasn't. But, the more I think about it, the more possible it seems. I wonder how many people I have trampled over in order to retain my status or to protect my church. And I probably never knew I was doing it.

And somewhere deep inside, that, quite apart from the theology, quite apart from my dissatisfaction with the social phenomenon of the church, was the personal reason for my decision, and all the resentment of those weeks was only there because I knew it reflected what I myself had become. Now I wanted to live a human life again, to relate, to react, to respond, to see needs, to share with others without being conscious of ministering at them. I wanted to be human, to be me. For my own sake, but also for the sake of the people I came in contact with.

And that, of course, was it. That was part and parcel of what I had been struggling with all through my ministry. And its root was still theological. With no doctrine of incarnation, of God actually being man, the church has no humanity. It simply does not understand, and therefore cannot practise, simple human caring. Sheer human concern, just caring what happens to people, does not crop up. We could talk about sharing and caring as long as I was one of the team. But I had put myself outside it. It was my decision.

It is not a spectacular story. I know that many people the world over have a much harder lot. But I do know what it feels like to have no home, and that is helpful. I also know what it feels like to be one of the church's outsiders. Jesus' main priority when it came to people was the outsider, the outcast. The church has never been very good at it – a stranger in church who dresses well, speaks well and expresses interest in the Mothers Union is all right. But once at the back of the church, I saw a tramp drinking meths. I saw a congregation of over a hundred, one by one, walk by and ignore him. Just one person offered him a cup of coffee. We have a tramp, too, at the theatre where I work at present. He was in the Green Room the other day, and a girl on the stage management staff had given him a glass of orange squash, and was chatting to him in a human, real way. That is the difference, and that is also what it is all about.

What is more frightening is that the story is not untypical. My mind shot back to people I had known: a theological college principal virtually hounded out because he was not willing to run a 'party' college; a priest whose wife had a sickness which had social repercussions, who was pushed out of his home with their two children, and the loving Christian community he had served were not allowed to know the reason why; a priest who had a nervous breakdown, moved to a village, and was specifically asked by the Bishop never to attend church there. Once you are outside, you are really outside.

For some reason, these incidents get covered up, even by those who have been the victims of the church's lack of humanity. Some still have loyalty to the church they have served, others want no truck with it at all. But I have become tired of defending the church against criticisms which I know from my experience to be true. And I have a suspicion that the vast majority of the population have never been fooled by the smooth talk from me or any other clergy. They know and have often seen that the church's treatment of people can be downright callous and rotten. No amount of covering up will bring those people back to church, only repentance by the organization and a determination to put things right, to start caring.

Which left me, after those weeks of homelessness, with a slightly different view of where I was going to stand in relation to the organized church. My first reaction was the inevitable emotional one of never wanting to set foot inside a church again. But I knew that would not last for long. The vision of what the church might be would reassert itself. But I do not wish to be trapped into making excuses for an organization of which I am not proud, which I believe to be fundamentally wrong in its thinking and its practice. I see myself rather as Ray Billington did more than ten years ago in *The Christian Outsider*, going to church when invited to do so, and perhaps from time to time slipping in at the back somewhere to retain something of its particular slant on the vision.

I do not know quite what I expect to happen. What will happen to me is something that I have at last decided to make my own responsibility. But what will happen to the churches? Do they have a future? Am I getting out of the kitchen because it is growing too hot? Or am I leaving a sinking ship?

As I see it now, the churches have a number of options. They could pull themselves together, and it would need to be done at every level. It would mean looking at the Bible again for what it says rather than what they think it says. Even those who claim to take it literally manage to manipulate it to their own ends. That looking must take place among the theologians, the parish priests and those in the pew. It will mean accepting things like 'You shall not kill' and 'Do not worry about tomorrow', to take two random examples, as meaning exactly what they say, and not hedging them about with qualifications. At the theological level, it will mean paying attention to those who doubt and question and criticize as well as those who produce tracts on traditional themes.

It would mean a great deal of swallowed pride – denominations giving up their prejudices and uniting for reasons of mission. It would mean, yes, the ordination of women and the remarriage of divorcees – it would mean taking people seriously, and what they believe God is for them. It would mean taking political stands, sometimes against the tide of public opinion or fashionable causes, and putting men and money and resources into the places where they are needed. It would need a total restructuring of ministry; far less parish priests, and more in the working and leisure situations where the 'flock' really spend their time. To pull themselves together would require a massive overhaul and an upheaval that the churches are not prepared to undertake. I detect in many places a wish for reform, but not the will.

Perhaps people like me, however disillusioned, should stay there and fight. For many years, it looked as though the best place from which to change the church was from within. But to be a parish priest with those priorities is now to be labelled 'trendy'. An actor I know who is also a church member sees me as the ultimate 'trendy vicar' – left-wing, radical, flying in the face of tradition. 'I bet you loved it,' he said. 'They all do, sticking their necks out.' But I was able to point out that I had left because I did not love it. I found no joy in the charge of trendiness. I am interested in truth. I wish to look at God's world without blinkers on, to see what is happening at the edges of my vision. In a sense, he is right. While most of the church establishment fights to preserve the *status quo*, those who resist have become not only loud, but a caste on their own. I do not wish to belong to them either. Reform of the church will not come from within its ranks, because, like all establishments, it has ways of dealing with potential reformers, categorizing them, even adulating them, certainly rendering them ineffective.

Another option the churches might take, and this might even in time develop from the first, is simply to elect to die. It might be done in a defeatist spirit, just calling it a day, admitting that the church's effect is now minimal. Or it might be done in that spirit of Jesus which faces the cross knowing resurrection is on the other side. But that will only come from a complete reversal of its obsession with self-preservation. One of the most frightening features of any church is that if you wanted to empty it, you probably would not succeed.

Such options are grandiose in the extreme, and too much to hope for. It is much more likely that the churches will continue exactly as at present for a long time to come. They will continue to fight the age-old battles, and smooth over the sores of life. But they will slowly become less and less effective. Their divisions will become more and more obviously ludicrous, their ability to shy away from every political issue will become more evident, their lack of concern for oppressed minorities and outsiders will render them sterile. And congregations will go on declining, and less and less people will take any notice of what church leaders say. The church will go on, but as fewer people are involved, it will presumably also become less harmful.

A depressing picture? Not at all. There are, thank God, literally thank God, plenty of people and places committed to the priorities that the organized church has chosen to abandon. In the theatre itself, *Godspell* is still preaching the faith of joy and love, and *Jesus Christ Superstar* is still posing the theological questions. There are thousands of people committed to relieving the hungry, the homeless, the depressed, political prisoners. Community associations, self-help groups, encounter groups, councils for racial harmony and all the others are taking up the issues. The cause of Christ is not lost by any means. Human beings do care for other human beings – it is, and will increasingly become, a matter of looking in the right places.

8

Another Way

I had known from way back that there were other ways. My experience at Cambridge of a personal link between the theatre and my faith was locked in my memory. It was never so much the superficial links between the church and the theatre – the presentation, the dressing-up, the oratory. It was something much more internal, and something much more to do with community. Harry Williams once wrote that to be a Christian was to live on the evidence of one's highest experiences. I knew that many of my own highest experiences were specifically 'religious'. They had occurred in that context, choruses around the camp fire, youth services in the parish church, my ordination, the funerals of some particular people. But I knew, too, of other experiences, which, although in a different context, had the same quality, and for me, most were related to the theatre and the arts – the first time I heard the first act of *La Bohème*, seeing the moving spotlights in Sadlers Wells first English production of *The Merry Widow*, playing in Brecht's *Galileo* at school, reading Dover Wilson's spellbinding interpretation of *Hamlet*.

This other set of experiences had more power and more breadth than the strictly 'religious' ones; they ranged more widely over different worlds and different emotions. They could not survive on their own, they risked becoming diffuse. What seemed to be needed was a balance, mind and emotion crossing uncharted ideas and feelings, and at the same time the figure of Jesus making his simple demand of love. That balance was through my ministry the one I tried to preserve. It led me often to using contemporary literature within the ancient structure of the Mass, to expressing religious belief in dramatic terms, in ministering pastorally to those in the theatre and entertainment.

And as the structures of religious organization seemed to close in and restrict, so flashes of light happened in other places. I directed Pinter's *Old Times* – it is a tight piece for three actors, and its intensity and its truthfulness led the four of us to discover many new things about ourselves and each other. Before a small audience, it sent a tingle up people's spines like electricity. As chaplain to a local night-club, I saw Charles Aznavour perform. His words and music may appear grudging of reality, but they have integrity. He is a consummate artist in cabaret, his blend of technique and feeling are amazing, and he guides his audience with great power into his feelings of anger and love of life.

And, above all, the people. Some friends I had retained from my locked memory. Others I set out to recover. Others I discovered in the theatres and the clubs and the local drama groups. Some talked of God, others of love. But they talked, they felt, they opened. Their business, and their linked existence, was about love and life and death, the articulation of hopes and fears, the very things that the church sought to organize into being. So I spent some time, talking and listening, in pubs, on commons, on the phone trying to pick up the atmosphere of what I was being told. Until I decided that the locked memories, the flashes of insight had once again to be tested out.

Since I laid eyes on my first Equity card and my first professional contract, I have in a sense been neither disappointed nor elated. It was as I expected it, and felt I had come home. I had underestimated how much I already knew, how much the ways and attitudes of the theatre had been part of my blood for so long.

The first self-evident feature of the theatre is its community, the fact of being a company. Very few theatres now keep a resident company complete over more than one production. This has to some extent destroyed a valuable link between theatre and community, but it does mean that the company that is in a theatre at any given time has a transient and flexible quality. We know before we start that the relationships we are going to make are primarily working relationships and only last for a matter of weeks. Those relationships thus take on a volatile nature. We are, for those weeks, totally dependent on one another, we have to learn very quickly and without inhibition some of the most deep things about one another. But knowing all the time that the company, the community, is doomed to be broken apart. It is in direct contrast to the endless posing of community in the church. Here the 'fellowship' has to exist, not because the concept is good, but because there is a show to do. There is no time, no energy for talking, or posing, or pretending.

I was present at a row between a director and a stage manager. The director had wanted to try something technical that evening, but the stage manager had sent the rest of his staff home to avoid paying them overtime (mean, but understandable!). Words were exchanged, and the stage manager walked out in a temper. Within five minutes, he was back, the two were sitting together. The director kicked the other under the foot to ask 'Are we friends?' They got down to discussing the point in question. When I left my last church, one of the churchwardens and the lady who did the cleaning were not speaking to each other. God knows how long and tortuous their reconciliation would be, if it ever happened at all. The church has lost any sense of a job to be done. It is the immediacy of a task to be fulfilled that is the stimulus of a theatre company.

That task crosses without question all those barriers that to the church seem so impenetrable. People need each other, not because it is their philosophy of life, but because their mutual dependence is self-evident. The actor cannot function without the electrician, the electrician cannot function without stage management. It all has to happen as planned, because we are relying on the others to do what they have to do, and they are relying on us. There is no other way it can work. This means, at the simple social level, a wide variety of types and classes of people involved. The amateur theatre is rather a different animal – it tends to become much more easily a group of middle-class people using their off-duty skills. But in the professional theatre, we are really talking about professional carpenters, and electricians and maintenance men sharing responsibility with those who might consider themselves intellectuals or aesthetes. The various organs of the body function together in the way that St Paul meant.

The class, the type, is not related to the job to be done. Within the strictly acting company of the first professional show I did, there was at one extreme a middle-aged actor, a former president of the Oxford University Dramatic Society, who believed that the show we were doing was a savage attack on Edwardian society: and at the other, a girl in her mid-twenties, brought up in the East End of London, who had never been trained, but discovered she could sing and dance. She told us stories of the ritual beatings her father gave her, and she still lived with her boy-friend in a council flat where she was brought up.

On stage, the waves of dependence and relationship are even more important. The actor who is not in some degree sensitive to what is being said and done around him sticks out like a sore thumb. He has to watch and listen – an inflection from someone else may be slightly different, and will require a slightly different response. Any number of permutations and imponderables may arise. And ironically enough, although the actor is, *par excellence*, the one creating a role, it is not a role behind which he can hide. He is continually exposed to himself, his own feelings and technical ability, exposed to his fellow-actors, and to the audience. Unlike the parish priest, he cannot retreat behind one costume and allow everyone else to adapt to his role. His role is actually being created, formed and re-formed by everything around him.

Even from the start, he is not being asked to take on a role for himself, but rather to delve into, explore the personality of someone different from himself, the ideas and visions of another, which may even run directly contrary to his own. And yet from within himself, he had to find those bits which are in sympathy with, which understand the character, his motives and his feelings, and it is these bits that he uses to flesh out, round the performance and make the character his own. The character has to be approached with humility, and also with considerable self-awareness. I know of no priest who approaches his parishioners demanding of himself that degree of sensitivity.

The technique, once set up as an ideal, becomes, I imagine, difficult to un-learn, and becomes part of the person. Which, together with the knowledge of mutual dependence, for me at least makes actors among the most sensitive, caring and generous people I have met. They are also good listeners. It is intrinsic to their job to be interested in other people, and to be aware of the vibrations that they are sending out. In the working situation, it shows in caring about trampling on each other's lines or laughs. There is almost a tradition that if one actor has 'thrown' another, cutting short one of his lines, mistiming a gesture on which the other relied, or anything of that kind, then he goes to the other's dressing-room to apologize. Often the other has not even realized that a mistake was made. It doesn't matter. The relationships must be whole, the fact that we are caring about each other and not scoring points off each other, must be clear. It is part of the actor's way of life.

It leads to a feeling of support and friendship that is remarkable. The welcome that I felt I received as a newcomer to the profession, not to mention tolerance of my early blunders, was unlike anything I had experienced in any church or parish. It was in direct contrast to what we were experiencing at home as we moved out of the vicarage. The support is sometimes company-wide, sometimes between particular individuals who find that for the time being, and at this particular time, each is exactly what the other needs. From this, I assume, springs the theatre's reputation for moral laxity. But these passing relationships may or may not have sexual connotations, in fact more often not. They are merely anarchistically temporary, but none the less creative, or real, or useful for that. And, at the end of the day, they are still part of some larger purpose.

I paint a massively ideal picture, of course. No human being can be that caring and supportive all the time, especially if it is a small company away from home, working intensely at close proximity. There are strains, there are cracking points, there are 'off' days. Which is why the actor has also to learn to put up with other people's weaknesses and failures, moods and faults. I found I had to learn, in a way that being a priest had never taught me, when to offer advice, when to cheer someone up, and when to just shut up and leave them alone.

How much we can read into the life-style of a company I am not sure. I suspect I am not making any claims for the theatre that could not be made in varying degrees for a dozen other professional situations. All I have discovered since leaving the full-time ministry, and which in truth I suspected before, is that there is a great big world out there, where people are already practising those arts of living towards which the church still struggles. And, to me, the ethos, the structure of the theatre seems very close to the free-wheeling ministry of Jesus and his friends in Galilee.

The church, of course, claims a higher role, a fuller charge than a group of people engaged on a common task. The first disciples were, after all, called men who were turning the world upside down. There have been, there will be, many words spoken and written on the role of the theatre in society. Some will say it has no such role. Actors are on a self-indulgent ego-trip. I think, in point of fact, that that is true. I became an actor because I wanted to do it. But I think many other professions are on every bit as much of an ego-trip as the actor: the teacher, the industrial tycoon, and I would even include the social worker and the clergyman. Some people get their kicks from making a fortune, others from the warm glow of being a needed and respectable member of society. It strikes me that the actor's self-indulgence may be a great deal less dangerous than many others, and less likely to be gained at the expense of his fellow-man. And most actors would, I think, admit to self-indulgence, which is half-way to turning his indulgence to some creative use.

In being part of a company performing one of the world's great plays to the best of its ability, one is inevitably inspiring, giving some new vision, new dimension to those who see it. One actor I know who was performing an Ibsen play told me that if it made one couple in the audience at one performance look again at their own marriage, then he had done a useful job. It will not always be as elevating as that. But there is also no sound on earth like that of an audience laughing. The play may only be skilful nonsense or a magical cheat, and yet it may take a gathered group of people out of their hum-drum lives into a world of delight and laughter. It may not inspire, it may only excite or enthuse or create dreams. It may only make people happy. But happiness and laughter are no small things.

The theatre rarely sets itself up in a social role or, if it does, it usually looks rather foolish. The church, of course, makes social pronouncements as often as possible (though carefully worded so as not to actually have any effect) and so looks foolish most of the time. And yet, strangely enough, it is very often the plays of one generation that subtly affect the attitudes of the next. The ideas, the attitudes somehow filter through to a society that never visits a theatre. Osborne's *Look Back in Anger*, for example, at the end of the fifties, is obviously and repeatedly noted as a revolution in the theatre. I imagine that a tiny minority of the population at large actually saw it then. And yet many of that play's ideals and priorities and hatreds became the norm of a whole generation in the sixties. Maybe they would all have come out anyway, maybe Osborne was doing no more than sensing the mood. But he did also articulate it, fuel the flames. I am not making a case for or against that particular play. It merely serves as an example. The pattern goes on weaving and filtering. If a play or a production or a performance has 'truth', if it is sensing the aspirations or ideals of those for whom it is performed, then I believe that in time, it can begin to change things.

One social phenomenon will illustrate the possible results of the ethos and purpose of the theatre while the church still struggles in its cage – that of homosexuality. One friend of mine has been wanting to be a priest in the Church of England for many years. He is gay, and unlike all the other gay clergy (and there are a large number) he has stated his gayness before presenting himself for ordination – he does not wish to be a hypocrite. This, of course, has presented the church authorities with a terrible problem. They say they want to love and accept him, but they do not wish to condone what many Christians still regard as a sin. They have tried to persuade him to keep his mouth shut on the subject, to be a hypocrite. He has been a licensed lay worker in two dioceses, and one Bishop took the brave step of making him a deacon. But as the natural time for his ordination to the priesthood arrived, they all got cold feet again. He has been given the sack by his vicar and colleagues, and the Bishop has refused to ordain him. The reason, he was told, has nothing to do with his gay sympathies or his left-wing politics. It is apparently to do with his inability to handle human relationships. The truth is, of course, that he handles them too well – he insists on being himself and real, and championing the causes of oppressed minorities. He is very dangerous to the church and a threat. Ordaining someone like that to the priesthood would be drawing attention to the inability of the church to deal with that social phenomenon. Refusing to ordain him, and the clumsy, despicable way in which his brother clergy have let him down and ruined his career, also reveals their 'inability to handle human relationships'.

I have been working recently with an actor who is very much the same kind of person – unashamedly gay, totally unpromiscuous and exceptionally good at talking to and listening to other people with considerable gentleness and dignity. On the night he left the company, the director of the theatre came to say goodbye. As he went out, the actor called after him 'Give my love to Liz' (the director's wife). The director called back 'And to Jonathan' (the actor's partner).

It could be, it should be, as simple as that. I think Jesus thought it was.

9

Alternatives

So the decision was made, and after all the talking and thinking, I had given up full-time ministry in the church and
become an actor. Two things, as it were, remained. One was a
very personal feeling of privilege that, although I was chang-
ing my career at this stage, I was still going into a job that I
wanted to do. My mind automatically recalls those who do
not have that privilege, who are able only to do the job that
lies to hand because, somewhere in the system, their freedom
of choice has been restricted. And yet, at the same time, I
wonder to what extent it might be possible for any human
being to enter the world he chooses to enter. It might be part
of the process of cutting free – at the end of the day, why
should anyone spend the greater part of his time engaged in
something that brings him no pleasure, no satisfaction? There
is a social problem here – if there are opportunities for everyone, it is perhaps not known that they exist. The turning-
point for me came when my will took over the practicalities. I
could have reasoned myself out of it at any point. But, somewhere along the line, I could see no valid reason why I should
not do exactly what I wanted to do. In one sense a selfish
move, of course, but in another sense, the knowledge that I
am doing the job I wanted has provided a firmer basis for

every other aspect of life. It may be that part of the process of setting people free is to discover quite simply what they want from life, and help them to achieve it, whatever the apparent costs and risks may be.

The other item left over was a more practical one. A priest is, the church always told me, a priest for ever. Priesthood is not simply a job, but a state of being. I could resign my job, I could stop being a 'parson', I could earn my money elsewhere, but I remain a priest of the Church of England, not only trained to be so, but ordained and commissioned in a solemn sacrament, authorized still to preach, to officiate. Unless, of course, I took the further step of resigning my orders, turning my back on the whole of the last fifteen years of training and ministry. One part of me was, of course, prepared to do just that. Within weeks of my departure, the deficiencies of the church assumed their true perspective. It has, for me, castrated any theology that might have led to its salvation, to its finding a creative role in our world. It has become pompous, corrupt and hypocritical, and yet so smooth and middle class as to cover it all up, like someone I once heard described as 'veneer all the way through'. Totally committed as it was to the right-wing of politics, there was no way I could be identified with this particular organization. I was not even prepared to concede that an organization in Jesus' name could exist. How could I conceivably remain one of the church's priests?

On the other hand, I had been trained to think theologically, I had in the years of baptizing, marrying, burying, visiting, preaching, planning worship, picked up certain expertise, certain beliefs about the way things might be done. And I had also approached the church with, for want of a better phrase, a sense of vocation, a desire to explore and represent the ways of Jesus to the world. And those were things that I had no wish to throw away. What I was about to try out, in a downright practical way, was what I had been hoping for over many years, an alternative meaning for Christian ministry, and specifically priesthood. It is tempting to describe what I look for as an alternative structure in which the gospel could be expressed. But 'structure', of course, is the impossible word. The very nature of the ministry I want is that it should be unstructured, free, something much more akin to Jesus' own wandering ministry in Galilee, and something that carries no risk of being systematized into any patterns of worship and conduct. Is this, in a sense, what the lay people I had been serving were doing all the time? Am I seeking only a lay ministry? No, because the orthodox churchman returns to base, as if the unstructured world were somehow deficient by virtue of its lack of structure. He uses, the church encourages him to use, the structured life of the church as a bastion against the world. And that is exactly the area in which I am quibbling. The gospel begins for me with the mammoth statement, 'God so loved the world . . .' The world is good and loved by God. We do not need to protect ourselves against it, we need rather to enter it, and by turns discover God in it and reveal God to it. Hence my search, in a world where the God/man distinction has been collapsed, where no man can be called an irreligious non-believer, for an infiltration, a real one, by those who have found Jesus to be the source of the joy and hope that the world already knows. Call them 'Christians' if you want. Or not, as you please. It really doesn't matter any more. What does matter is that, in and through the world, in a totally unstructured, un-selfconscious way, the values are being upheld, the signposts are marked, the search for meaning goes on. It will not be done by a group set apart from the rest, only by truly secular people. There will be a great deal of interweaving of different

83

individuals, different groups, drawn together not by a set of beliefs codified for eternity, but by a common sharing of the values and signposts that concern them at that particular moment, for that particular issue.

And sometimes amid the weaving, there may be a place for some individuals who can express and articulate the search, who make it their business to read what needs to be read, to take public stands, to talk when asked to do so, to hammer through some intricate relationship that is holding up the search, sometimes even to mark, to ritualize the high points of love and life and death. Perhaps a priest. Not one of them, representing a dying and corrupt establishment, but one of us, working with us, laughing and loving with us, yet known by us to have thought along particular lines, accumulated particular skills.

In the theatre, the idea of expressing my priesthood leaves me various options. At one level, the actor is already a priest, articulating and drawing out many things that men and women deeply believe. Peter Brook, in his remarkable book *The Empty Space* devotes a chapter to the theme of the holy theatre, making visible the invisible, performing all the time the fact of incarnation. Both in his way of working and in the presentation of the finished product, the actor is already feeling through the world of ideas and their effect on human relationships. He is already a dealer in visions and dreams, and how best to communicate them. As an actor, I already find myself doing what I believed I was called to do as a priest.

That does not allow, of course, for a ministry within the theatre, only a one-way process from the theatre to the world. Within the church, the Actors Church Union has over the last fifty years been the main organ of a ministry to those within the profession. It has a pattern of chaplains to theatres all over the country – while an actor is at any one theatre, the chaplain is his parish priest. It's organized, of course. My own interest led me, obviously, to be one of the chaplains for several years. Each week, I would go to the theatre to meet the company. I usually related quite well to some, and was given a polite brush-off by others, which I always regarded as fair enough. I never got to know any as well as I wanted, I was always conscious of imposing myself on them, and I knew always that there were many things about their existence that I neither shared nor understood. There must be, I always felt, a deeper, more real way of being a priest to these people. At least I took these part-time chaplaincies seriously.

It was some time before I actually realized that this highly organized pattern of chaplains making contact with the profession from theatre to theatre was a pipe-dream, and as fraudulent as the rest of the church's ministry. I state as conscious exceptions a handful of colourful and hard-working priests who are known throughout the theatre. But by and large, from town to town, theatre to theatre, the chaplain is a non-person. I need not have felt guilty if I only visited once a week. Most like to have their name on the call-board, but never visit at all. I began to ask touring companies how often they had met the chaplain – tours of six weeks, ten, sixteen. 'No, no,' the reply kept coming back, 'you're the first chaplain we've met.'

Another aspect of my priesthood was to break through that barrier, to be not a stranger who knocked on the door of the dressing-room, but a friend and a colleague. I don't know whether it is laziness on someone's part or whether all pastoral care of the company is in my hands but I have, at the time of writing, worked in one theatre for three months, and I have never seen or met the chaplain. To my knowledge, he

85

has not set foot in the building. Maybe, as I say, I am being left to be the worker priest.

Is that what I am? A worker priest? In a sense, yes, as long as it means that I seek to express my priesthood in my work, among my working colleagues, and as long as it does not mean that I have to go scrabbling back to the organization on a Sunday to take a few services, as long as I do not have endlessly to justify my existence as an actor to the church, or to defend the church to my colleagues. I work, and I am a priest. For the present, I wish to acknowledge those two facts, and let them be.

So what form, if any, what weaving patterns, do I even envisage an ordained Christian ministry will take within a profession like the theatre? What form, for that matter, could they take in any profession, if it is really outside the cloistered structures? Are there areas of life, portions of such training and expertise that I happen to have, that can still be used? Can we find genuine alternatives for ministry, liturgy, spirituality, witness, or at least new ways of doing them that do not demand returning also to credal statements, hierarchical structures, and the trap of priestly role and status?

What the church pompously calls the 'pastoral' aspect is inevitably there. There are still people. One friend of mine left full-time ministry to go into religious broadcasting, and a mutual friend of ours sadly said that it was a great shame, because he was so 'good with people'. I do not know who he thought our friend was going to be working with now! The people I work with know that I am a priest, and I believe I have had some conversations with some of them, been asked advice on some issues, that would not have happened otherwise. I am now, no less than before, called upon to show pastoral concern. Indeed, rather more than before, since I am with these people most of the time, and moreover, I have to do it rather better than before, since they know me better – it is less easy to cover up my blunders and hypocrisies. In this context, the 'pastoral' aspect might lead rather more naturally into the liturgical – the deliberate expression of the most crucial moments of our mutual existence. My current programme biography ends: 'He is an Anglican priest, and is retaining his orders so that he can bury his friends in the theatre!' Expressed as a joke, of course, but it also makes sense. How much more sensible for an actor to be married by someone he actually knows, for his children to be baptized by someone he has worked with, for the dead to be buried by a friend and a colleague. I can see every case for continuing to perform these occasional offices. They may be far more occasional than in the parish, but they would have a thousand times more reality. And maybe, one might even recover the reality of a few friends gathering spontaneously with bread and wine to celebrate that we are alive and free at all. Maybe one day I shall celebrate Communion again, only this time it will be Holy Communion, holy because it is real, and has integrity and truth.

On the subject of Christian witness, the media people who interviewed me at the time were fascinating. They all wanted to know where, as a priest, I was going to stand on the questions of rude jokes and nude performances. Their obsession with that area may reflect less on them, and more on the way the church has witnessed to its Lord. It has sold Jesus as the one who objects primarily to sexual innuendo and display of the human body. In fact, Jesus has almost nothing to say about either – and one or two of his own parables would strike some churchmen as being in dubious taste. And the theatre, of course, has its own reputation for total moral depravity. An actor came with me to one television interview and when I was asked how I intended to approach 'the salacious world of the theatre', he laughed and said 'The chance would be a fine thing.' The depravity simply does not exist, or at least no more than anywhere else and, as elsewhere, those who play fast and loose with other people's feelings are not the most respected members of the profession. It may come as a surprise, but most human beings do have rather high moral standards. To the question of doubtful jokes and nude scenes, I have developed a stock reply, which I regard as thoroughly Christian: that if we are going to talk about obscenity, let us talk about the real obscenities – hunger, homelessness, injustice, oppression, bitter loneliness. It is in these issues that real salaciousness lies. It is from them that the Christian will recoil in disgust, and in comparison a blue joke, a sexual theme, a naked human body, is frankly neither here nor there.

And if the church has ever wanted to make a witness, to take a stand, it should always have been on these far more important issues. In fact, it will talk about anything – baptism policy, ordination of women, the wearing of vestments, the whole gamut of massive irrelevancies – rather than actually make a blistering attack on the third of the world that allows the other two-thirds to rot, or a political party that sets out to stir up racial hatred on our own doorsteps. Granted, there are token gestures, there are individual Christians who have these things high on their priorities, but they are over and above the call of duty. Christian Aid, for example, is by no means central to the life and work of every church: it is an optional extra in those places where the vicar pushes it. Maybe as a priest outside it would be possible to do what the churches refuse to do, bring these things to the centre. In any walk of life, and no less in the theatre, there are people deeply involved in relief agencies – Oxfam, War on Want, there are those committed to the release of political prisoners through

Amnesty International, there are those who are Samaritans. There are the people whose commitment and goodwill we might be harnessing, using, demonstrating. And there are, and will be, other areas to be opened up. The theatre where I am is currently playing *Sizwe Banze is dead*. The National Front threatened to disrupt the first night: the company know which side I, as a Christian, am on, and they know my enthusiasm for that particular play. It does not count for much, I have no role or status now, but it remains an act of Christian witness in an area of life that matters.

Part of the witness that I have also to learn is to become intelligently involved with Equity. Like all trade unions, its concern is the well-being of its members. I have not yet got the measure of its political wings, but I cannot describe the relief in finding that even a faceless union actually cares how many hours a week I work and whether I am having proper time off. Relief, that is, having left a concern which professes so much, and yet neither knows or cares about such things, where clergy have heart attacks at forty through over-work, and where you can be sacked with no redress.

Pastoral care, liturgy, ethics, witness – and so to the last great priestly function: the spiritual life. Surely this whole aspect of Christian life is the one that still needs to be developed within the specifically Christian community, or else abandoned altogether.

I take as my text 'Jesus went into the hills from time to time to pray.' The hills and the spontaneity of it are the centre of his spirituality. And in a world where the incarnation has happened, where God is man, where there is no such thing as a godless man, it makes every kind of sense. Each person is spiritual, just as each person is sexual. No man can afford to repress instincts as deep as those. All psychiatrists know the damage done by the repression of the sexual drive. We have nowhere near estimated the results of crushing the spiritual part of man, the part that estimates love, the part that searches for meaning in the universe, the part that fears death. In the world outside the church is exactly where the doors and windows need to be flung open – no, more gently than that, where each persons needs to be quietly led to the God who has become him or her. And that will only be done in a context of growing awareness.

Yes, I will pray – by myself, for others, with others if they wish it. But not in structures and patterns, not making it a world on its own, but in their hills, from time to time, in the open air of thought, where all sorts of other winds blow, and where we can all breathe. Naturally, the New Testament will be the basis of this spiritual growth, not because it is sacred, but because it really does say everything. And it will not be read with preconceived notions, with all its later distortions written in. Let us look at it again, the stories of Jesus, the amazing ideas of the early Christians. It needs all its own doors opened – you can see why the church hardly reads it any more, hardly ever really reads it.

And from a basis of mutual prayer, and from the visions of the New Testament, the spiritual search, the growth of each soul's life, will lead out and away all over the place. You can see it happening all round, and it is right that it should. It leads to awareness of the body, to Yoga, to meditation, to techniques of self-knowledge, to diets and vegetarianism, to new understandings of the great landmarks of our culture, to Zen; some options for some people, others for others. It means reading and exploring all sorts of ideas and possibil-ities, and so all sorts of being and feeling and doing. As long as the search is on, as long as we keep looking, and there are others to open doors for us, as long as we open doors for each other. Have you read . . . ? Have you seen . . . ? Do you care about . . . ? What do you mean by . . . ? We must never stifle the spiritual life again; we must not lock it up again in new churches and new creeds. And if I am sure of that in my own new life of rehearsal rooms and dressing rooms and pubs, I believe I can remain a priest, and of Jesus' kind.

I do not, having made my decision, regard the theatre as an alternative church, though it has elements of it. The real alternatives can and will be explored anywhere. Anywhere, that is, where people are functioning freely and openly, where the restrictions have been taken off. For me, one step towards that entailed, as my butcher observed, 'working like the rest of us'.

That move, towards being a working colleague rather than holding a position of status was, I think, always central to my understanding of ministry and priesthood. Jesus himself has no time at all for those who are set up as religious status symbols. His whole notion of leadership is based on the principle that the true leader is the one who serves. Many clergy will quote that saying of his, without seeing that their very existence as a separate caste belies it. If Jesus was saying anything, it was that you cannot witness to the love of God, you cannot truly help or serve your fellow-man from a position of superiority or privilege. And I discovered at last that for ten years, just by the shape of the job I had, that was exactly what I was trying to do.

The flat that, after several months, we found to live in was, although not in the same town, of exactly the same design as many I had visited any number of times in my own parish. And the first time I climbed the steps to my own front door, I realized how, when I had climbed steps like those before, I had always done so in a patronizing way. I never meant to – indeed, I prided myself on not, like most clergy I knew, being pompous and patronizing to those in the parish. I wanted human, real relationships then, too. But there was no way I

91

could avoid it. As long as I was going home to a large vicarage which I did not have to pay for, and as long as I was in a position of respect and authority simply because I was 'the vicar', there was no way in which I could honestly relate to those people or they to me. It was a doomed exercise.

All this reflected not a whit on my Christian faith. I have never, as people like to say, 'lost my faith'. Rather the reverse – within the organized church, I found no time or inspiration to practise my faith. The issue revolves around not the truth of Jesus or the New Testament, but around what concrete expression that truth is to take in the world. The church buildings, the ritual of liturgy, the pattern of priesthood are concrete enough, but they no longer express the truth of Jesus, only the status and privilege of the church. Whereas the New Testament does make it clear how that truth is to be made real, and it will be in exactly these alternative areas – in individual men and women asking the spiritual questions and finding the truth of God in themselves; in caring again about the quality of each relationship, whether a deep one or a chance acquaintance; in political action, either at the level of local needs or by involvement in the major issues of the world. It will always be veering from one direction to another. It cannot be focussed on one building, or one priest, or one piece of organized worship.

The whole world is God's, and it is wonderful, chiefly because he has loved and redeemed it. Christ is for all men, without exception or distinction. The Christian is the one who will set out to prove it, and really mean to do so.

So how, finally, do we present this Jesus to a world in fear of meaninglessness? The concept of incarnation is, to say the least, rarified. The confession 'Jesus is Lord', the ancient confession which is the key, rings like jargon in our ears. The gospel, the good news, from the tradition, remains true – Jesus of

Nazareth, born AD 4, died AD 32, rose from the dead and is the sole means of salvation for men. But if you put it like that, no one will be glued to the edge of their seats, waiting for more pearls of wisdom. The sum total of the frustration and fears that surround the church is to accept that these are the 1970s, and that this Jesus business has got beyond a joke. It is as if Christ is still the answer, but to a question that nobody is asking.

In the bluntest practical terms, if by 'being a Christian', you mean going to church to get bored out of your mind; if you mean saying a form of words that you do not believe in to someone that you are not sure is there; if you mean having religious disciplines to make you feel better; if you mean being a puritan or a prude, following a moral code based on the four-letter word 'Don't', and above all, not enjoying yourself – if that is what it all means, then I have no wish or need to be a Christian either. If that is the Way, I side with those who do not follow it. But those of course are the marks of the followers of Nobodaddy.

Here in the seventies, where we are, there are different questions. There is half a world dying of hunger, there are the homeless, there is marriage breakdown, there are drugs, there is a god called Growth, there is mental illness, vagrancy. There are five million black Rhodesians with no control over their own lives, there is racial conflict in our schools, there are well over a million unemployed. These are facts, they are the real situations of men and women in our generation. Look at what is being done for such people. The religion of Nobodaddy has nothing to offer them. But try to tell me that the care and compassion of Jesus Christ exhibited in the people of God is unnecessary, and I would laugh in your face. It is exactly the challenge, the vision and the love of God-is-man and man-can-be-God that is more violently needed now than it has been for centuries.

93

The people of God has always been, and still is, a nation at war. And war has no use for the sloppy or the uncommitted. It needs those with guts, men and women of the future who will get involved with the world they live in, love it and, if necessary, get crucified for it. It may well be that the next decade will, as it were, sort out the men from the boys, those who are committed to standards and values, above all to life, from those who remain in the rut of religious obeisance. There is no generation gap – only a gap between the living and the dead, those with guts and those without, those who stand for something and those who fall for anything, those who care about the real, and those who care about the trivial. The first task of the followers of this Jesus is to become de-trivialized, to stamp out in themselves the trivial, the dull, the wet and the boring.

Some years back, I was asked to plan a youth service along with some young people. I asked them, as I thought I should, what they cared about, what was most important to them. Foolishly, I expected them to say 'the homeless' or 'Vietnam' or some other current cause. In the end, one girl said 'Me - that's what I care about most – me.' It may appear selfish, but she was absolutely truthful. The hub of a community that does not care, that has no guts, is the individual who does not care for himself. Part of the fear is that the individual has ceased to value himself. He has no guts because he lacks self-confidence. He goes for a drink, or works late, or watches television from six till midnight, because he does not fundamentally believe that he is of any value. He says 'No' to the world, because deep down he feels that the world is saying 'No' to him.

And it is to that point that God-is-man and man-can-be-God carries its strength. It is the statement that nothing is more holy, more infinitely precious than a human life. That the man in the pub is the object of love by the universe. He is able to be de-trivialized, to enter the way, to show care, to proclaim the Lordship of Christ over the fear that it may all be nothing, only at the point where he knows that he is accepted for who he is, that totally, as he is, he is real, that he matters, that the whole of creation, that the ends of the universe, look to him, to his real personality, and utter 'Yes' – a huge, magnificent, resounding 'Yes'. That is what Christians mean by the love of God.

There is a moment of such realization brilliantly painted in John Whiting's play *The Devils*. Grandier, the renegade priest, is returning from having administered the sacrament to a dying man. As he approaches his own town of Loudun, he reflects on his life and is overwhelmed by his own value.

GRANDIER: And then, and then, I created God! I created him from the light and the air, from the dust of the road, from the sweat of my hands, from gold, from filth, from the memory of women's faces, from great rivers, from children, from the works of man, from the past, the present, the future and the unknown. I caused him to be free from fear and despair. I gathered in everything for this mighty act, all I have known, seen and experienced. My sin, my presumption, my vanity, my love, my hate, my lust. And last I gave myself and so made God. And he was magnificent. For he is all these things.

I was utterly in his presence. I knelt by the road. I took out the bread and the wine. Panem vinum in salutis consecramus hostiam. And in this understanding, he gave himself humbly and faithfully to me, as I had given myself to him.

SEWERMAN: You've found peace.

GRANDIER: More. I've found meaning.

SEWERMAN: That makes me happy.

GRANDIER: And, my son, I have found reason.

SEWERMAN: And that is sanity.

GRANDIER: I must go now. I must go to worship him. . . .

In a sense, this book is a commentary, no more, on that speech, on that kind of experience. The only answer to the 'Yes' of the universe is 'Yes' in return, to the world, to the universe, and thus to God. Only 'Yes' makes a life liveable. Jesus of Nazareth is Lord, necessary for the seventies as long as man is necessary, as long as you are necessary. Let the swords and guns be taken up, and the cross of Christ, and let a new church be born to build a more just, more free, more peaceful, more loving world.